The Gingerbread Lady

Maureen Stapleton as EVY MEARA & Ayn Ruymen as POLLY MEARA.

THE GINGERBREAD LADY

A NEW PLAY

by Neil Simon

RANDOM HOUSE · NEW YORK

Photographs by courtesy of Sy Friedman-Zodiac

Library of Congress Catalog Card Number: 72–163468
Standard Book Number: 0-394-47310-8

Manufactured in the United States of America by Haddon Craftsmen, Scranton, Pa.

2   4   6   8   9   7   5   3

FIRST PRINTING

THE GINGERBREAD LADY *was first presented on December 13, 1970, by Saint-Subber at the Plymouth Theatre, New York City, with the following cast:*

(In order of appearance)

JIMMY PERRY	Michael Lombard
MANUEL	Alex Colon
TOBY LANDAU	Betsy von Furstenberg
EVY MEARA	Maureen Stapleton
POLLY MEARA	Ayn Ruymen
LOU TANNER	Charles Siebert

Directed by Robert Moore
Setting by David Hays
Costumes by Frank Thompson
Lighting by Martin Aronstein

THE SCENE

The action takes place in a brownstone apartment in New York's West Seventies.

ACT ONE

A late afternoon in mid-November.

ACT TWO

Three weeks later—about 9:00 P.M.

ACT THREE

The following morning.

Act One

The scene is the third-floor apartment in a brownstone in the West Seventies. It consists of a living room, a bedroom and, to the left, a kitchen. The rooms are fairly large, with high ceilings and what were once very nice wood panelings, now painted over. In the mid-thirties and forties this was a great place to live. The furniture is very good and probably very attractive but one could hardly tell any more; it has fallen into disrepair. Against the wall there is a small, battered piano that is covered with photographs, all of a theatrical nature. A stack of mail is on the table.

A man's sheepskin coat is draped over a chair. From the kitchen we hear the faucet running and a man humming. He comes out with a vase he has just filled with fresh flowers. JAMES PERRY *is in his early forties, portly and probably homosexual. Probably but not obviously. He wears slacks with a dark blue turtleneck sweater. He first goes to the window and peers out and down, looking for the arrival of someone; then he turns back and looks for a place to put the vase. He tries the piano, changes his mind, then settles on the coffee table. It doesn't please him much.*

JIMMY   I hate it. *(The doorbell rings. He looks at his watch nervously, then crosses to the door and asks without opening)* Who is it?

MANUEL *(Offstage)*   Groceries.
          *(*JIMMY *opens the door and glares at the delivery boy,* MANUEL, *who is Spanish and about twenty. He is holding two large grocery bags in his arms)*

3

JIMMY   Where were you? I thought you went out of business. Put them in the kitchen, please.

MANUEL   *(At doorway)*   Mrs. Meara live here?

JIMMY   Yes, Mrs. Meara lives here. Would you please put them in the kitchen.

MANUEL   *(Not moving)*   Is fourteen dollars twenny-eight cents.

JIMMY   Fine. Terrific. That's a charge. Just put them in the kitchen.
> (JIMMY *starts to walk away but notices that the boy is not moving*)

MANUEL   Mr. D'Allessandro say to me I mus' have fourteen dollars and twenny-eight cents.

JIMMY   No, you don't understand. Mrs. Meara has a charge account. *Charge—account!* Do you know what that is?

MANUEL   *(Nods)*   Tha's a charge account.

JIMMY   That's right. It's an account and you charge it. I don't live here. I'm a friend of Mrs. Meara. You charge it to her account.

MANUEL   Mr. D'Allessandro say to me eef they say to you, eet's a charge account, you say to them eet's fourteen dollars and twenny-eight cents.

JIMMY   Do you want me to get on the phone and call Mr. D'Allessandro? What's the number?

MANUEL   The number? The telephone number? Ee's seven-six-six-something, I don't know, I never call them . . . Eef you speak to Mr. D'Allessandro, he's gonna say to you eet's fourteen dollars and twenny-eight cents.

JIMMY *(Irritated)*   I don't have to call Food Fair, you know. They have canned goods in Bohack's, too.

MANUEL   Bohack's is nice. My cousin works for Bohack's. They all the same, you know.

JIMMY *(Glares at him)*   . . . I don't have fourteen dollars and twenty-eight cents. I have no money on me.

MANUEL   Oh, well, tha's okay. I'm sorry.
(He turns)

JIMMY   Where are you going?

MANUEL   Back to Mr. D'Allessandro.

JIMMY   Wait a minute. I'll look. *(He takes his wallet from his back pocket. The boy smiles at him.* JIMMY *turns his back so the boy can't see into his wallet. He takes out one bill)* I have ten dollars.

MANUEL *(Shrugs)*   I leave you one package.

JIMMY *(Glares more angrily)*   Wait here. *(He starts for his sheepskin coat, notices that the boy has edged inside a step or two)* That's far enough.

MANUEL   Wha's a matter, Meester, you afraid I come inside, I rob you house? I don' rob no houses.

JIMMY   I don't care what you do, just wait there.

MANUEL   I got a good job, I don' have to rob houses.

JIMMY *(Half to himself as he goes through his pockets)*   Yeah, in the daytime. *(He takes a passbook out of his pocket, along with some loose dollar bills. He holds the book in one hand and counts money as he crosses back)* How much was that again?

MANUEL   Same thing, fourteen dollars twenny-eight cents. *(The boy puts down the packages.* JIMMY *takes out four singles and hands them to the boy, but in the process he drops the passbook on the table. The boy picks it up and looks at it)* Oh, I use to have thees. Unemployment book. You unemployed, Me-ester?

JIMMY *(Grabs it back)*   None of your damned business. Who asked you? You've got your fourteen dollars. You can leave now.

MANUEL *(Holds out his hand)*   And twenny-eight cents.

JIMMY *(Reaches into his pocket and takes out the change. He hands it to the boy, one coin at a time)*   Ten ... fifteen, twenty-five, twenty-six, twenty-seven, twenty-eight cents. *(The boy looks at it, and nods his head in agreement)* That's all. There's no tip. I don't live here. I don't tip where I don't live.

MANUEL   I don' wan' no tip. You ain't even got a job. I don' need your tips.

JIMMY   And I don't need your goddamned sympathy. You're very fresh for a delivery boy.

MANUEL   Wha's a matter, you don' like Spanish people?

JIMMY   Who the hell said anything about Spanish people? *You're* the only one I don't like. Will you please leave now?

MANUEL *(At the door)*   I know the kin' of people *you* like, Meester.

(He makes two kissing sounds with his pursed lips)

JIMMY *Get out of here! (The boy smiles and rushes out, the door closing behind him.* JIMMY *bolts the door, then crosses to the grocery bags, still fuming)* I wouldn't live in this neighborhood if you paid me . . . *(He picks up the bags and starts for the kitchen)* Can't say a thing any more, everyone is so goddamned race conscious . . . Lousy spic! *(He goes into the kitchen. We hear the rustle of the paper bags as the phone rings.* JIMMY *comes out with a can of coffee in his hand and crosses to the phone)* Hello? . . . No, she's not, I'm expecting her home any minute. Who's calling, please? . . . Well, in regards to what? . . . Oh! Well, I'm sure Mrs. Meara hasn't paid her phone bill intentionally. She's been away sick for the past ten weeks . . . But you're not going to cut it off, are you? She'll pay it as soon as she gets home . . . Fourth notice already, my goodness . . . But you must realize she's good for it. I mean this is Evelyn Meara, the singer . . . It must be in by Tuesday, yes, I'll tell her that. Thank you very much, I appreciate that. *(He hangs up. To the phone)* Wait three years to get one but you rip 'em out fast enough, don't you? *(He starts opening the can. The front doorbell rings.* JIMMY *turns and looks at the door. He is extremely anxious. He puts the can of coffee down on a chair, wipes his hands on his pants and goes to the door. He calls out without opening)* Who is it?

TOBY *(Offstage)* It's us. We're home.

> *(*JIMMY *starts to open the door, but it doesn't work, since he's forgotten that he bolted it. He tries to unbolt it but has a little difficulty at first)*

JIMMY *(Calls out)* Wait a second, I'm so damned nervous. *(He finally opens it, and* TOBY LANDAU *enters. She is a very pretty woman, in her early forties—but you'd never believe it. That's because she spends most of her waking hours trying to achieve that effect. She is well dressed in a smartly tailored suit. She carries a large, heavy, but not very elegant suitcase)* Look at me, I'm shaking.

TOBY *(Entering)* Don't complain to me. I just spent four hours in a taxi on the Long Island Expressway. Look out the window, you'll see a very rich cab driver.
(She looks around the apartment)

JIMMY Where is she? *(He looks out the doorway)* Evy? Where's Evy?

TOBY She's saying hello to a neighbor . . . I thought you were going to clean the apartment. Didn't you say you would clean the apartment for Evy?

JIMMY I tried rearranging the furniture, but it always came out like a bus terminal in Passaic. Where is she? Is she all right?

TOBY Yes, but you're going to be shocked when you see her. She lost forty-two pounds.

JIMMY Oh, my God.

TOBY I will tell you right here and now that a rest home for drunks is the most depressing place in the world.

JIMMY I never thought she'd last it out. I'm so nervous. What do I say to her? How do I act in front of her?

TOBY You hug her and love her and, above all, you must trust her.

JIMMY I'll kill her if she ever takes another drink . . . Where the hell is she?
(We hear EVY's *voice just outside the door)*

EVY (*Offstage*)   I'm out in the hall. Are you ready?

JIMMY   Ready.
(EVY *enters, wearing a mink coat and carrying books*)

EVY   All right, say it, I'm gorgeous, right?

JIMMY   Oh, my God, I don't believe it. Who is she? Who is this beautiful woman?

EVY   It better be me or I'm out twenty-seven hundred bucks.

JIMMY   Am I allowed to hug you?

EVY   You're allowed.
(JIMMY *rushes into her arms and hugs her. He feels her*)

JIMMY   It's true. It's gone. Forty-two pounds are gone. Where did it go to?

EVY   You want it? It's in the suitcase.

JIMMY   I can't get over it. It's like talking to a stranger. Somebody introduce me.

TOBY   Jimmy, this is Evelyn Meara. Remember? She used to sing in clubs?

JIMMY   That fat lady? Who used to drink a lot? Use foul language? No. This is a nice skinny woman. You put a dress on her, you can take her anywhere.

EVY   I don't want to go anywhere. I want to be right here in my own apartment . . . Oh, it's so good to be home. (*Looks around*) Jesus, it looks different when you're sober. I thought I had twice as much furniture.

TOBY   Will you sit down? (*To* JIMMY) She won't sit down. She stood all the way in the taxi coming home.

JIMMY   You must be starved. When did you eat last?

EVY   I had chicken salad in July. I'm not hungry.

TOBY   The doctors told me she worked harder than any
patient there. Even the nurses were so proud of her.

EVY   It's the truth. I was the best drunk on my floor
. . . (*Looking at the sectional*) Christ, now it's coming back
to me. I threw the other half of this out the window.

JIMMY   I want to make you something. Let me make you a
tongue and Swiss on toast and a pot of coffee. Sit down.
I'll be five minutes.

EVY   I thought my mother lived in Ohio. Leave me alone.
I tortured myself to lose forty-two pounds.

TOBY   Jimmy, stop it, you'll get Evy nervous.

JIMMY   I'm worried about her. If someone doesn't make it
for her she doesn't eat.

EVY   There's plenty of time to eat next year. I'm all right.
I'm home. Let me enjoy myself.

JIMMY   Who's stopping you? (*To* TOBY, *softly*) She look all
right to you? (TOBY *nods*) Is there anything she has to take?
Pills or anything?

TOBY   Just some tranquilizers. She has them in her bag.

JIMMY   But nothing heavy? No serious stuff?

TOBY   Just a mild sedative to help her sleep.

EVY   (*At the kitchen door*)   If you doctors want to be alone, I
can go back to Happy Valley . . . What are you whispering about?

JIMMY   We're not whispering. We're talking softly.

EVY   You were whispering.

JIMMY   We were not whispering. We were talking softly.

EVY   Why were you talking softly?

JIMMY   Because we don't want you to hear what we're saying . . .

TOBY   Jimmy's worried about you, that's all.

EVY   If he's worried, let him worry a little louder. I can't
stand whispering. Every time a doctor whispers in the
hospital, the next day there's a funeral.

JIMMY   I'm sorry. I'm sorry.

EVY   It took ten weeks to cure me and five minutes for you
to drive me crazy.

TOBY   Jimmy didn't mean it, darling.

EVY   What are you blaming him? You were whispering
too.

TOBY   I had to. He whispered a question to me.

JIMMY   All right, can we drop it?

TOBY   I didn't even bring it up.

EVY   Jesus, I got along better with the nuts on Long Island.

JIMMY   I'm sorry, Evy. All right? I'm nervous I'm gonna
say the wrong thing. I don't know how to act in front of
somebody who just got home from the cure five minutes
ago.

EVY   You act natural. The way you always acted with me.

JIMMY   This is the way I always acted with you.

EVY   Yeah? Well, maybe that's why I started to drink.

TOBY   My God, what a homecoming.

EVY   *(Wilts a little)*   Hey, listen, I'm sorry. Maybe I am
nervous . . . Don't pay attention to me. Jimmy, you know
what I'd love more than anything else in the world? A
tongue and Swiss on toast and a pot of coffee.

JIMMY   Do you mean it?

EVY   I dreamt of it every night. First I dreamt of sex, then
a tongue and Swiss on toast.

JIMMY   I'll bring you the sandwich. The rest I can't help
you with.
   (He exits into the kitchen)

TOBY   *(Looking at herself in the mirror)*   And what can I do,
Evy?

EVY   You can stop looking at yourself and give me a cigarette.

TOBY   You *are* nervous, aren't you?

EVY   I hated that place so much I used to save up matches,
planning to burn it down. It was a goddamn prison. And
then when it came time to leave I was afraid to go . . . I
suddenly felt comfortable there . . . Can I have my cigarette, please?

TOBY   That's almost a whole pack since we left the hospital.
Are you sure they said it's all right to smoke?

EVY   Once you pay your bill and check out, they don't care
if you get knocked up by a dwarf. *(Takes the cigarette and*

smokes) I thought I'd have a million things to do once I got home. I'm here six minutes, I'm bored to death.

TOBY   You've got to give yourself time, Evy. And then you're going to start your life all over again and you're going to grow up to be a beautiful wonderful person like me.

EVY   What's that? What's that crap you're putting on your face?

TOBY   It's a special crap that protects the skin. Have you noticed you've never seen pores on me? As long as you've known me, have you ever seen a single pore on my face?

EVY   I've never even seen your face . . . Who are you, anyway?

TOBY   A woman can never be too pretty. It's her feminine obligation. I love my looks, don't you?

EVY   You're gorgeous. If you went bald and lost your teeth, you'd still be cute-looking. Leave yourself alone.

TOBY   I can't. Isn't it terrible? I'm obsessed.

EVY   You remind me of the psycho in the room next to me. She used to shampoo her eyelashes every night. Thought all the doctors were in love with her. An eighty-seven-year-old virgin screwball.

TOBY   What a sweet story . . . You just going to sit there forever? Aren't you going to unpack or something?

EVY   Unpack what? A pair of pajamas and a bottle of mineral oil? Besides, I'm never going in that bedroom again. I ruined half my life in there. The next half I'm playing it safe.

TOBY   I understand perfectly. But how will you get to the bathroom?

EVY   Over the roof and down the pipes. Just worry about your face, all right?

TOBY   I can worry about both. I wish I could stay with you tonight.

EVY   Then why don't you stay with me tonight?

TOBY   I have to meet Martin at Pavillon for dinner. It's business—I distract the client.

EVY   Some friend you are.

TOBY   Don't say it like that. I'm a wonderful friend. I'm sensitive. You want me to be hurt?

EVY   Don't pout. You'll crack your make-up and start an avalanche on your face.

TOBY   Anyway, Jimmy can stay with you tonight.

JIMMY   *(Sticks his head in through the kitchen window)*   Jimmy has an audition at five forty-five.

TOBY   You said you'd be free tonight.

JIMMY   I was until the audition came up. I have to eat, you know.

TOBY   Can't you cancel it? For Evy?

JIMMY   I wouldn't cancel it for Paul Newman.

TOBY   Oh, God, Evy, I'm sorry. What will you do tonight?

EVY   I'll turn on television and stand stark naked in front of Merv Griffin. What the hell do you think I'm going to do all alone?

TOBY You could call Polly. She's probably home from school by now.

EVY I'm not ready to see my daughter yet, thank you. What I'd really like to do is move the hell out of this dump.

TOBY Then why don't you move?

EVY Because, dumb-dumb, I still pay a hundred and twenty dollars for three and a half rooms. It's on a sublet from Mary Todd Lincoln.

TOBY You can borrow from Marty and me until you go back to work again.

EVY Work? Singing in clubs? The last job I had was two years ago in Pittsburgh. I broke the house record. Fell off the stool seventeen times in one show.

TOBY That's old news, I don't want to hear about it.

EVY I shared a dressing room with a female impersonator who had the hots for me. I think we made it, but I forget which way.

TOBY You don't have to sing in clubs. There's television— Martin knows people in advertising. You can be a cat in a tuna fish commercial, you'll make a fortune . . . I've got to go.

EVY So soon?

TOBY I'm afraid so, Marty's waiting.

EVY Just gonna dump me here like a basket case, heh? I thought you were going to stay and grow old with me.

TOBY Don't be silly. I'm never growing old . . . I won't go if you're really desperate.

EVY When have you known me when I wasn't desperate?

TOBY Never. If you need me I'll be at Martin's office and then at Pavillon. Can I send you anything?

EVY How about the headwaiter?

TOBY Armand? He doesn't go for women.

JIMMY *(Entering with a tray with cups of coffee)* Send him anyway, we'll find something for him to do.

TOBY Evy, this may be one of the happier days of my life.

EVY Toby, if you didn't come to pick me up today . . .

TOBY I told you. I'm always way the hell out on Long Island early Thursday mornings. Tell me once more how pretty I am.

EVY Helen of Troy couldn't carry your compact.

TOBY I believe you, Evelyn. I really do. I'll call you from the restaurant. *(She goes to the door; stops)* Evy . . . say it just once more.

EVY Say what?

TOBY What you promised me in the taxi.

EVY *(A pause)* I will be a good girl. For ever and ever.

TOBY Oh, Christ, I'm going to cry—there goes my make-up.

> *(She exits quickly.* EVY *turns to* JIMMY*)*

JIMMY You skinny bastard, I'm so proud of you.

EVY   Is that why you didn't visit me once in ten weeks?

JIMMY   I can't go to hospitals, you know that. I pass out in hospitals. If I ever get hit by a car I tell them, "Take me to a drugstore, never a hospital."

EVY   It wasn't a hospital. It's a sanitarium for drunks.

JIMMY   They had white shoes and cotton balls, that's enough for me. *(He hands her a cup of coffee)* Didn't I call you almost every day? Didn't I send you popular novels?

EVY   Queen Alexandra and her hemophiliac son? Couldn't you send me a sex manual, for chrissakes?

JIMMY   I'm sorry I was nice to you. Next time I'll just send you a get-sober telegram.

EVY   How much do I owe you for the groceries?

JIMMY   We got 'em free. I had an affair with the delivery boy.

EVY   Next time *I'll* answer the door. Give me the bill.

JIMMY   Don't be ridiculous. Where would I get money?

EVY   You were just in a show.

JIMMY   That was in October and we ran two nights and were closed by the police. Please don't ask me what I had to do naked with six people on the stage.

EVY   Was it something sexual?

JIMMY   I couldn't tell, I had my eyes closed . . . That is the goddamned last time I will ever take my clothes off in public. Not only have I not worked since then, I can't even get a lousy date any more. You know what I did to keep alive? God is my judge, I worked in Bonwit's selling snakeskin toilet-seat covers, on my mother's life.

EVY *(At the window, looking out)* I don't see any men on the streets. Little boys, fags, hippies, but no men.

JIMMY What kills me is that I'm so good. I'm such a good actor I can't stand it. But I'm too late. Show business is over this year. There will be no more entertainment in the world after June. Maybe you'll see a person whistling or humming on the street, but that's all. I was born too talented and too late. What are you doing at the window? Who are you looking for?

EVY Nothing.

JIMMY You look tired. Why don't you lie down for a while?

EVY I don't want to lie down.

JIMMY You've got to lie down sometime.

EVY That's an old wives' tale. I've known people to stand for years at a time . . .

JIMMY *(Lost in his own problems)* I won't get this job tonight. They'll turn me down. I'm auditioning for some nineteen-year-old putz producer who has seventy-five thousand dollars and a drama degree from Oklahoma A&M . . . First time he walked into the theater he fell off the stage, broke two ribs . . . Some chance an intelligent actor has today . . . Oh, God, I want to be a star so bad. Not a little star. I want to be a big star with three agents and two lawyers and a business manager and a press agent, and then I'd fire all of them and get new ones because I'm such a big star. And I'd make everyone pay for the twenty-two years I poured into this business. I wouldn't do benefits, I wouldn't give money to charity. I would become one of the great shitheels of all time. Isn't that a wonderful dream, Evy!

EVY *(Looks around)* She didn't leave any cigarettes. Stupid dumb broad.

JIMMY *(Takes a crumpled pack out of his shirt pocket)* Here. Take whatever I have. My money, my blood, whatever you want—only calm down, because I don't trust you when you get nervous.

EVY I just made up my mind: I don't like you.
(*She takes one of the cigarettes*)

JIMMY You never liked me. For fifteen years it's been a one-sided friendship. I'm the one who always worries about you, picks you up off the floor, puts you to bed, feeds you—and for what? Christmas you gave me the one lousy album you made in 1933 . . . Well, I'm through. I can't take it any more. You're skinny and sober, take care of yourself now.

EVY How'd you like a big wet kiss on the mouth?

JIMMY How'd you like a tongue and Swiss on toast? Sit down, it's ready.
(*He starts for the kitchen*)

EVY *(Yells)* Jimmy, will you stay here and talk to me!

JIMMY *(Stops)* What do you want to talk about?

EVY Anything, dammit, pick a subject.

JIMMY Why don't you ask me, Evy? Why don't you get it over with and *ask me?* . . . No, I have not seen him or spoken to him, all right?

19

EVY *(A pause; she nods)* All right.

JIMMY I'm lying. I saw him at the bar in Downey's last week. I don't think he's doing well because he had one beer and ate all the pretzels in the dish . . .

EVY Was he alone?

JIMMY Yes. I know because when he left I watched him through the window hoping he'd get hit by the Eighth Avenue bus . . . What else do you want to know?

EVY Nothing. I was curious, not interested.

JIMMY Oh, really? Is that why you keep staring out the window? Is that why you won't go into the bedroom? What are you afraid of, you'll see his lousy ghost sitting on the john doing the *Times* crossword puzzle? . . . Go on. Go in the bedroom and get it over with, for chrissakes.
(EVY looks at him, then goes into the bedroom. It is quiet a moment. Then we hear EVY from the bedroom)

EVY How'd you get the Bloody Mary stains off the wallpaper?

JIMMY I hung your bathrobe over them.

EVY *(Reenters living room)* You know what I'll do? I'll repaint the room white. The whole bedroom white, top to bottom. Walls, floors, bedspreads, shoes, stockings, everything white. And I'm going to forget everything that ever happened in there and I'm going to become one happy, TV-watching, Protestant, square-assed lady, how about that?

JIMMY Nixon'll be thrilled.
(The doorbell rings. EVY looks startled)

EVY   Are you expecting anyone?

JIMMY   I don't even live here. Should I answer it? They're
just going to ring again. *(It rings again)* See!
(EVY *nods. He opens the door. It's the Spanish delivery boy
with one package in his arms)*

MANUEL   I forget the soda. Six cans Coca-Cola, six cans
Canada Dry ginger ale. Two dollars, forty cents.

JIMMY   I paid you before, didn't I?
(He tries to grab the package)

MANUEL   You paid me for las' time, you dint pay me for this
time. Two dollars and forty cents, please.

JIMMY   *(Angry)*   Did you tell D'Allessandro that Mrs.
Meara is going to take her business somewhere else?

MANUEL   He don' care. He say, "Take the Coca-Cola somewhere else."

EVY   *(Steps forward)*   What's wrong?

JIMMY   There's nothing wrong. *(To the boy)* Wait out there.
I'll get your money.
(JIMMY *takes the bags and goes into the kitchen)*

MANUEL   I don' wanna come in your house.
(EVY *steps out into the center of the room so that she is in
view of the boy for the first time)*

EVY   Jimmy, don't leave him out in the hall like that. *(To*
MANUEL) That's all right, you can come in.
(The boy looks at her and smiles)

MANUEL   Oh. Okay.
(He steps in)

EVY *(Smiles at him)* I'm Mrs. Meara.

MANUEL Oh, yes? Hello, Mrs. Meara, nice to meet you. *(He nods his head a few times, looks her up and down)* I brought you six cans Coca-Cola, six cans Canada Dry ginger ale. Okay?

EVY I don't see why not. That's a charge. And put fifty cents on for yourself.

MANUEL Oh, thank you very much.

EVY You're welcome.

MANUEL But I need two dollars, forty cents. Mr. D'Allessandro say to me—

EVY I know what Mr. D'Allessandro said to you. It's all right. You tell him Mrs. Meara is home and will take care of everything by check again. Will you do that?

MANUEL Yes. I'm going to tell him that. But he's going to tell me not to tell him that.

EVY What's your name?

MANUEL Mr. D'Allessandro.

EVY No, *your* name.

MANUEL *My* name? You want to know *my* name? Manuel.

EVY Manuel?

MANUEL *(Nods)* Manuel. Yes, that's my name. Manuel. Eet's Spanish.
   (JIMMY *comes out of the kitchen*)

EVY I haven't seen you before, Manuel. What happened to the other boy?

MANUEL   Pablo? Pablo got married and is now work in a better job. Bloomingdale's.

EVY   Really? He seemed so young.

MANUEL   They don' care how old you are in Bloomingdale's.

EVY   I mean to get married.

MANUEL   Oh, Pablo is twenny years old, same as me.

EVY   You're twenty?
       (JIMMY *has been watching this with consternation*)

MANUEL   Tha's me, twenny.

EVY   Well, let's hope that you get married and find a better job too, Manuel.

MANUEL   Eet's okay eef I find a better job, but I don' wanna get married. I'm okay now, you know what I mean?

EVY *(Smiles)*   You mean you have lots of girl friends, is that it?

MANUEL   Sure. Why not?

EVY   Well, you tell Mr. D'Allessandro I will send him his check the first thing every month. Will you do that?

MANUEL   The first thing every month. Tha's what I'm gonna tell him.

EVY   And put fifty cents on for yourself. I don't have any change just now.

MANUEL   Tha's awright . . . I come again. You take care of me another time—you know what I mean? (*There is a slight suggestiveness in his tone that does not go unnoticed by* EVY *or*

23

JIMMY) Goo'bye, Mrs. Meara. (*To* JIMMY) Okay, Meester, eet's okay now, we're good friends again, all right?
(*He winks at* JIMMY *and exits, closing the door behind him*)

JIMMY *(Yells)* Jesus Christ! Why didn't you invite him in to listen to your Xavier Cugat records? Are you crazy?

EVY Oh, come on, he's a delivery boy.

JIMMY I saw the look he gave you and I know what he wants to deliver.

EVY I'm not in *that* kind of trouble yet . . . maybe in a few weeks, but not yet.

JIMMY I can't trust you. I can't trust you alone for ten minutes.

EVY I can be trusted for ten minutes.

JIMMY I know you, Evy. I wouldn't leave you with the Pope during Holy Week . . . Haven't you had enough trouble this year?

EVY I've had enough for the rest of my life. For Christ's sake, I'm not going to shack up with a delivery boy. I don't even have a quarter to give him a tip.

JIMMY You'll charge it like everything else.

EVY Oh, God, Jimmy, I really love you. You don't know how good it is to have somebody worried about you.

JIMMY Well, I hate it. I have enough trouble worrying about me. I'm forty years old and I can't get a job with or without clothes any more. If you want to carry on with Pancho Gonzales, that's up to you.

EVY (*Puts her arms around* JIMMY)   Of all the stinking people in this world, you sure ain't one of them.

JIMMY   Well, I'm glad you finally realize all the others are stinking.

EVY   Why don't you marry me?

JIMMY   Because you're a drunken nymphomaniac and I'm a homosexual. We'd have trouble getting our kids into a good school.

EVY   Give me a kiss. *(He kisses her lightly)* Come on. Give me a real kiss. Who the hell's gonna know?
     (He kisses her with feeling)

JIMMY   God will punish us for the terrible thing we're doing.

EVY   Don't get depressed but you get me very excited.

JIMMY   I don't have to stay and listen to this kind of talk. *(Breaks away from her)* I've got to go. If you promise to behave yourself, I may be nice to you when I'm a star.

EVY   We could live together in Canada. They don't do sex in Canada.

JIMMY *(Putting on his bag)*   Stop it, Evy, you're confusing my hormones. I'm late.

EVY   Jimmy!

JIMMY *(Stops)*   What?

EVY   Nothing. I just love you and want to thank you for being here today.

JIMMY   Don't thank me, just pray for me. Pray that I get this show because I think it's the last one in the world.

EVY   Will you call me the minute you hear anything?

JIMMY   It's off-Broadway, there are no phones. *(On his way out)* I bought you that Stouffer's macaroni that you love. And some Sara Lee cheesecake. And I made you enough coffee until February. Will you remember to drink it?

EVY   Drinking is one thing I remember.

JIMMY   And get some sleep.

EVY   I promise.

JIMMY   And if José Ferrer shows his face again, don't open the door. The only groceries he's bringing next time are his own.

> *(He exits, closing the door behind him.* EVY *turns and looks at the empty apartment with full realization that she is alone, alone again for the first time in months. She picks up her suitcase and literally throws it into the bedroom)*

EVY   All right, don't panic, we'll take it one night at a time. *(She looks around, puffs up the pillows on the sofa, then sits down on it)* . . . And that's it for the week! *(She crosses to the piano, plays a few notes of "Close to You," then sings the first line)* . . . Thank you, thank you . . . For my next number, Ed Sullivan and I will make it right here on this stage . . . *(She sighs heavily. She is fighting to keep from losing control of herself. She looks at the phone, goes over to it quickly, sits and dials . . . Into the phone)* Hello? . . . Is Miss Meara there? . . . No, not *Mrs.* Meara, *Miss!* . . . Oh? How long ago? . . . Well, when she gets in, would you please tell her— *(Suddenly a key turns in the lock and the front door opens.* POLLY MEARA *stands there with one large, heavy suitcase.* POLLY *is seventeen, pretty, with long straight hair and no pretensions. She wears blue jeans, a sweater and a jacket. There is a long and emotional pause as the two stare at each other across the room. Then* EVY *speaks into the phone)*—never mind, I just heard from her.

    (She hangs up and stares at POLLY*)*

POLLY   I don't want to get your hopes up, but I have reason to believe I'm your daughter!

EVY   No, you're not. *My* daughter would have called first ... *(No longer able to contain herself)* ... You rotten kid, you want to give me a heart attack? *(They rush to each other, arms around each other in a huge, warm embrace.* EVY *squeezes her tightly)* Oh, God, Polly, Polly ...

POLLY   I was hoping I'd get here before you. But I was late getting out of school. Of all damn days ...

    (They break the embrace. EVY *wipes her eyes)*

EVY   Okay, I'm crying. You satisfied? You just destroyed a helpless old woman ... Well, why the hell aren't you crying?

POLLY   I'm too happy. I can't believe it. My God, look at you.

EVY   What do you think?

POLLY   You're gorgeous. Skinniest mother I ever had. I can wear your clothes now.

EVY   What size dress do you wear?

POLLY   Five.

EVY   Tough, kid, I wear a four. *(Wipes teary eyes again)* Damn, I knew this would happen. You weren't supposed to know I was home. I needed three days before I could face you.

POLLY I called the hospital this morning. You didn't think I could wait, did you?

EVY Neither could I. Oh God, give me another hug, I can't stand it. *(They embrace)* All right, if we're going to get physical, let's close the door. There's enough talk about me in this building.
(EVY *closes the door.* POLLY *goes to get the suitcase from in front of the door)*

POLLY I'll get that.
(She picks it up)

EVY Have you had dinner yet?

POLLY I haven't even had lunch. I was too nervous.

EVY I just loaded up for the winter. We'll have a food festival. Come on, take your coat off, let me look at you. Hey, what'd you do with your hair?

POLLY Nothing.

EVY I know. It's been three months. When you gonna do something?

POLLY Don't bug me about the way I look. I'm not that secure yet.
(She heads for the bedroom with the suitcase)

EVY I should have your problems. Where you going with that?

POLLY In the bedroom.

EVY What is it?

POLLY *(Looks at it)* Looks like a suitcase.

EVY Thanks, I was wondering. What's in the suitcase?

POLLY *(Shrugs)* Dresses, shoes, books, things like that.

EVY Why do you have things like that in your suitcase?

POLLY Well, otherwise they fall on the floor.

EVY All right, no one likes a smart-ass for a daughter. What's going on here?

POLLY Nothing's going on. Can't I stay?

EVY Tonight? You know you can.

POLLY Okay. I'm staying tonight.
  (She starts for the bedroom again)

EVY With all that? You must be some heavy sleeper.

POLLY Okay, *two* nights. Let's not haggle.

EVY Hey, hey, just a minute. Put the suitcase down. (POLLY *looks at her, then puts it down*) . . . Now look at me.

POLLY I'm looking.

EVY And I know what you're thinking. Oh, no, you don't.

POLLY Why not?

EVY Because I don't need any roommates, thank you . . . If you had a beard, it would be different.

POLLY I don't want to be your roommate, I just want to live with you.

EVY You lonely? I'll send you to camp. You have a home, what are you bothering me for?

POLLY You can't throw me out, I'm your flesh and blood.

EVY   I just got rid of my flesh, I'm not sentimental.

POLLY   I've already decided I'm moving in. You have nothing to say about it.

EVY   In the first place, idiot, you're not allowed to live here. It's not up to you or me.

POLLY   And in the second place?

EVY   I don't need a second place. The first one wiped us out. You live where your father tells you to live.

POLLY   Exactly. Where do I put the suitcase?

EVY   Are you telling me *your* father gave you permission to move in here with me?

POLLY   Right.

EVY   *Your* father?

POLLY   That's the one.

EVY   A tall man, grayish hair, wears blue suits, spits a little when he talks?

POLLY   Would you like to speak to him yourself?

EVY   Not sober, I don't. What does your stepmother think about this? What's her name, Lucretia?

POLLY   Felicia.

EVY   Felicia, some name. He must spit pretty good when he says that. Did she ever get that clicking in her teeth fixed?

POLLY   Nope. Still clicking.

EVY   That's a nice way to live, with a spitter and a clicker. Thank God he didn't get custody of me too.

POLLY   That's why I'm begging you to take me in. I can't do my homework with all that noise.

EVY   God's truth, Polly? He really said yes?

POLLY   He likes me. He wouldn't kid around with my life.

EVY   Why don't I believe it?

POLLY   We've been talking about it for months. He knows how hard you've been trying. He spoke to your doctor, he knows you're all right . . . And he thinks you need me now.

EVY   *Now* I need you? Where does he think I've been the last seven years, Guatemala?

POLLY   He knows where you've been.

EVY   And what about you? Is this what you really want?

POLLY   I've been packed for three years. Every June I put in bigger sizes.

EVY   You wanna hear something? My whole body is shaking. I'm scared stiff. I wouldn't know the first thing about taking care of you.

POLLY   I'm seventeen years old. How hard could it be?

EVY   I'll level with you—it's not the best thing I do. I was feeling very motherly one time, I bought a couple of turtles, two for eighty-five cents, Irving and Sam. I fed them once—in the morning they were floating on their backs. I don't think I could go through that again.

POLLY   I'm a terrific swimmer.

EVY   Jesus, the one thing I hoped I wouldn't have is a dumb daughter. What kind of influence would I be on you? I talk filthy. I have always talked filthy. I'm a congenital filthy talker.

POLLY   Son of a bitch.

EVY   I don't think that's funny.

POLLY   Well, I just got here, give me a chance.

EVY   What the hell is the big attraction? I thought we were doing fine with visiting days.

POLLY   When I was nine years old, do you remember what you gave me for Christmas?

EVY   An empty bottle of Dewar's White Label? I don't know, I can't remember yesterday.

POLLY   Don't you remember the gingerbread house with the little gingerbread lady in the window?

EVY   If you say so.

POLLY   I always kept it to remind me of you. Of course, today I have the biggest box of crumbs in the neighborhood. Come on, be a sport. Buy me another one this Christmas.

EVY   I don't know if I could afford it.

POLLY   What are you afraid of?

EVY   Of leaving you with the crumbs again . . . You know what I'm like.

POLLY   I've seen you drunk. Mostly I hated it but once or twice you sure were cute.

EVY You only saw dress rehearsals. I was very careful around you. A mother doesn't like to get too pissed around her own daughter. Am I supposed to say things like that in front of you? Pissed?

POLLY If you can do it, you can say it.

EVY There are other things I can't tell you . . . Ah, Christ, I might as well tell you. You knew about Lou Tanner.

POLLY I met him here a few times.

EVY Did you know we lived here together for eight months?

POLLY I didn't think he got off a bus in those pajamas.

EVY Jesus, at least have the decency to be shocked.

POLLY There's a sixteen-year-old girl who just left school because she's pregnant. You're forty-three. If you're not allowed, who is?

EVY How'd I suddenly end up with the Mother of the Year Award?

POLLY I don't want to judge you, Evy. I just want to live with you.

EVY You're seventeen years old, it's time you judged me. I just don't want you to get the idea that a hundred and eighty-three pounds of pure alcohol is something called Happy Fat . . . Many a night I would have thrown myself out that window if I could have squeezed through . . . I'm not what you'd call an emotionally stable person. You know how many times I was *really* in love since your father and I broke up? I met the only man who ever really meant anything to me about seven, maybe eight,

times. Mr. Right I meet at least twice a week . . . I sure
know true love when I see it. It's wherever I happen to
look.

POLLY You don't have to tell me any of this.

EVY *I do*, dammit . . . I want you to know everything,
Polly, before you make up your mind. I lived here with
that guitar player for eight of the happiest months of my
life. Well, why not? He was handsome, funny, ten years
younger than me, what more could a woman want? . . .
He sat in that chair all day working and writing and I fed
him and clothed him and loved him for eight incredible
months . . . And then that dirty bastard—I'm sorry, I'm
going to try not to do that any more.

POLLY Good.

EVY No, the hell with it. That dirty bastard. He walked
out on me in the middle of the night for an eighteen-year-
old Indian hippie. "Princess-Screw-the-Other-Woman"
. . . Wait'll she gets old and starts looking like the face on
the nickel. And he doesn't have a penny, not a cent. Well,
her moccasins'll wear out, we'll see how long that affair
lasts . . . But I sat at that window for six weeks, waiting
and hoping while I ran through two liquor stores in this
neighborhood alone . . . Finally Toby came in one day and
found me face-down in the bathtub . . . I woke up in a
sanitarium in Long Island, and the rest isn't very interest-
ing unless you like stories about human torture . . . But
I went through it and I'm here. And I figure, pussycat,
that I have only one more chance at this human-being
business . . . and if I blow it this time, they'll probably
bury me in some distillery in Kentucky . . . And if this
is the kind of person you'd like to live with, God has

cursed me with one of the all-time-great schmucks for a daughter.

POLLY *(Smiles)* How'd you like to come and speak at my school?

EVY *(Adores her for this)* I think I would rather have you than a mink coat that fits. *(She hugs* POLLY*)* You still want to take a shot at it?

POLLY After that story, I'd pay for a seat.

EVY Oh, no. If you move in, it's a whole new ball game. If you're going to live here with me, we turn this place into "Little Women." Clean sheets, doilies on the furniture, TV *Guide*, a regular American family.

POLLY And we can go to church on Sunday. By the way, what religion are we?

EVY I'll look it up. I've got it here somewhere . . . I'm going to get a job. Not in show business—a real job.
   (She starts pacing)

POLLY I get home from school at four, I could start dinners.

EVY Can you cook?

POLLY No, but I can get them started.

EVY Is that all you can do?

POLLY I can ride a horse.

EVY That's it. When we're starving to death, you're the one who rides for help.

POLLY Can I unpack now?

EVY   Yes, you can unpack now! . . . Holy Christ, Polly, I am suddenly so excited. How did I get so lucky?

POLLY *(Shrugs)*   Some people have it all.
(POLLY *starts into the bedroom with the suitcase*)

EVY   See what looks good in the kitchen, I'll put your things away.
(EVY *starts for the bedroom as* POLLY *starts for the kitchen. They pass each other on the way*)

POLLY   So far we're doing terrific.
(EVY *disappears into the bedroom.* POLLY *is in the kitchen. Both are offstage*)

EVY *(Offstage)*   What the hell do you have in here, Yankee Stadium?

POLLY *(Offstage)*   It's my record collection.
(The doorbell rings)

EVY *(Offstage)*   I see a lot of panties here but I don't see any bras. Don't you wear a bra?

POLLY *(Offstage)*   No. Am I missing a big thrill?
(POLLY *comes out of the kitchen. She looks toward the bedroom, but apparently* EVY *hasn't heard it.* POLLY *crosses and opens the door.* LOU TANNER *is standing there. He is in his mid-thirties, with scruffy, unmanageable hair, a full, bushy mustache, a dirty turtleneck sweater and light-tan desert boots, very worn. He is, despite his appearance, attractive.* POLLY *is shaken by his ill-timed arrival*)

POLLY   Hello, Lou!

LOU *(Looks at her, then past her into the room)*   Hello, Polly.

EVY *(Offstage)* I'm not going to ask you what these pills are for because I don't want to know and I don't want to hear.

LOU She all right?

POLLY *(Still shaken)* What? . . . Yes. She's fine.

LOU Can I come in?

POLLY *(Looks toward the bedroom worriedly)* Yes, sure. *(He steps into the room. She closes the door behind him)* How are you?

LOU I thought she'd be alone . . . Maybe I ought to come back later.

POLLY No. No, I'm sure she'll want to see you. *(Calls out)* Mother! . . . Someone's here.
> (LOU *stares at the bedroom door as* POLLY *eyes him nervously.* EVY *appears in the bedroom doorway. She has probably recognized* LOU*'s voice. She comes out of the bedroom and faces* LOU)

LOU Hello, Evy.

EVY *(Trying to be cool)* Hello, Lou . . .
> *(There is a moment of awkward silence)*

LOU You look fabulous.

EVY Thank you.

LOU How'd you lose so much weight?

EVY Sheer happiness.

POLLY *(This is no place for her)* I'll finish unpacking. I'll see you, Lou.

EVY   That's all right, you can stay.

POLLY   I'd rather not, if you don't mind. (*Nods at* LOU) Lou.

> (*She exits quickly into the bedroom.* EVY *and* LOU *stand there eyeing each other*)

LOU   I checked the hospital. They told me you were coming home today. Rough scene, heh?

EVY   No, I loved it. They showed movies Saturday nights . . . How's Pocahontas?

LOU   We split about a month ago.

EVY   Ah, that's too bad. What was the problem, couldn't she make it rain?

LOU   She couldn't make it, period. A lot of sexual hangups among the Cherokees. (*Looks around*) You going to offer me a cigarette?

EVY   No, but you're welcome to take a bath. You look like the second week of the garbage strike. You living indoors somewhere?

LOU   Eddie Valendo's on the road, I'm using his place.

EVY   I hope he left you food, you look a little shaky.

LOU   Musicians don't eat, Evy, you know that. We live on "soul."

EVY   Whose?

LOU   I wouldn't turn down a bottle of cold beer.

EVY   You asking or begging?

LOU   Is that what you want to hear? Okay, I'm begging.

EVY   I always knew you'd make it big some day. *(Hands him a cigarette)* Here. There's one left. Smoke it when you're older.

LOU *(Tries to grab her)*   That's my Evy.

EVY *(Pulling away)*   You are one, priceless, unbelievable bastard. You had to walk in here today, didn't you? You had to time it so you'd get me holding my nerves together with spit and coffee.

LOU   What'd you want me to do, phone you from a pay station in Walgreen's? "Hi, Evy, guess who this is?"

EVY   The only thing stopping you was the dime.

LOU   Come on, Evy, I walked seventeen blocks in borrowed shoes. Talk nice to me.

EVY   Like nothing ever happened, right?

LOU   No, it happened. We'll talk about it. But it's hard when you don't look at me. I get the feeling I'm suddenly left all alone in this room.

EVY *(Turns and looks at him)*   I know the feeling well.

LOU   I'll say one thing for the Indians. Generally speaking, they're not a vindictive people.

EVY   Really, Lou? What'd she do when you walked out on her? Ride into the sunset? Do a little sun dance? Wriggle and bounce her firm little body? You want to tell me about her tight little eighteen-year-old body, Lou?

LOU   Not particularly.

EVY Come on. Lay it on me. Talk that hip, colorful language you dig so much. Tell me your problems, Lou, you'll get a lot of sympathy from me.

LOU No problems, Ev. Nothing that can't be worked out.

EVY Lou, I'm forty-three years old and I'm trying to be a grown-up lady. The doctors told me I'm not allowed to drink any more or have affairs with thirty-three-year-old guitar players . . . I thank you for this visit. Now go home, find someone your own age and light up some Astro-Turf or whatever you're smoking these days.

LOU *(Smiles)* If nothing else, Evy, you have a way with a phrase. I used to quote you. Word for word. Of course, this dumb little Indian chick never saw the humor. We communicated in other ways. But whenever I needed a good honest laugh, I had to quote you, Ev. You weren't in the room, but you were there, you know what I mean?

EVY It's an image I think I'll cherish forever . . . Listen, Polly is here and I think we ought to cut this short.

LOU I want to come back, Ev. *(There is a pause)* Today, tomorrow, next week . . . but I want to come back.

EVY I see! . . . Would that be with or without meals?

LOU Maybe with a little humility. I'll scrape up whatever I can.

EVY I don't want you to steal just for me.

LOU There it is, Ev. That's what I've come back for. A little stimulation.

EVY Try a vibrator.

LOU Try letting up for two minutes. Take an interest, Ev, ask me how my work is coming.

EVY How's your work coming, Lou?

LOU Gee, it's nice of you to take an interest. I'm writing. I'm not selling anything, but I'm writing.

EVY *(Without emotion)* I am *enormously* pleased for you.

LOU You don't give a crap, do you? You never did give a good goddamn.

EVY That's too hysterical to be answered.

LOU Oh, you cared about *me.* I never questioned that. Affection, love, passion, you had it by the tonnage. All I had to do was look at you with anything less than indifference and you were ready to jump in the sack with your shoes on.

EVY Forgive me. Frigidity is not one of my major hangups.

LOU I could have been a counterman at Riker's, it wouldn't have made any difference to you.

EVY *Nothing* made any difference to me except you.

LOU You didn't give a damn if the stuff I wrote was good or not as long as it was finished. "It's terrific, Lou, now come to bed."

EVY You wrote it, you played it, I listened to it. Short of publishing it there wasn't a hell of a lot more I could do.

LOU You never really liked it, did you? You never thought I had any real talent, did you?

EVY I loved it. Everything you wrote I loved.

LOU   Bullshit.

EVY   That's a better way of putting it.

LOU   Then why the hell didn't you say so?

EVY   I had enough trouble getting affection from you without giving you bad reviews.

LOU   I can't believe it. You hated everything I wrote and you never said a word to me until now.

EVY   I'm sorry your ego is hurt posthumously. All right, I think you're very promising. I'll take a page ad in *Variety*, now leave me alone.

LOU   You know, Evy, you are the biggest ball-breaking insufferable pain-in-the-ass woman I ever met—and I'm standing here enjoying it . . . I'm cut up and bleeding from abuse and humiliation but at least I know I'm in the room with a living human being . . . *(Softening)* I haven't had a good all-out-fight like that in three months . . . I have also, in that time, not put down a piece of music worth the price of the paper . . . Maybe you're right. At best I'm mediocre. But mediocre is better than wasting good music sheets . . . Come on, Evy. The truth is, while I was here, I functioned. And when I functioned, you functioned.

EVY   Evy and Lou functioning: one of the great love stories of all time.

LOU   *(With some humor)*   Well, maybe not the greatest, just the most original . . . What do you say, Ev? Make a contribution to the world of serious music.

EVY   I already gave.

LOU   Christ, Evy, you want me to say it, I'll say it. I need you very badly.

EVY   For how long, Lou? Until you run off with the Chinese hatcheck girl at Trader Vic's?

LOU   Evy, I swear—

EVY   Don't make me any promises. I just left a hospital filled with people waiting for promises.

LOU   Come on, for chrissakes, you had that problem for twenty years before you ever met me.

EVY   No argument. I just don't want it for twenty years after.

LOU   What are you going to tell me, you're cured? You had buttermilk for twelve weeks and now you'll live happily ever after? . . . There's still a whole life to get through, Evy . . . I'm not coming in here offering you any phony promises. Sure, in six weeks I may find another cute-assed little chick, and in eight weeks they might find you under the piano with a case of Thunderbird wine. Then again, maybe not. Together, Evy, we don't add up to one strong person. I just think together we have a better chance.

EVY   What I need now is a relative, not a relationship. And I have one in there unpacking.

LOU   Who are you kidding?

EVY   She'll be here in the morning. That's good enough for me.

LOU   The mornings have never been your problem.

EVY   We were just going to have dinner. I'd ask you to stay but it's just the immediate family.

LOU   Well, it was kind of a slow afternoon, I just thought I'd ask . . . I'm really glad to see you in good shape, Ev . . . Take care of yourself.

EVY   That's the general idea.

LOU   *(At the door)*   You still have ten seconds to change your mind. *(He waits. No reply)* My, how time flies.
(He opens the door, about to go)

EVY   Lou! *(He stops, turns; there is a pause)* Will you call me sometime? Just to say hello?

LOU   *(Looks at her)*   Probably not.
(He turns, goes, closing the door behind him. EVY stands there a moment. The bedroom door opens. POLLY comes out)

POLLY   I didn't hear a word . . . But can I say something?

EVY   Only if it'll make me laugh . . . Are you unpacked yet?

POLLY   It would take me two minutes to put it all back.

EVY   If you're unpacked, then wash your hands, set the table and light the stove. It's dinner time.

POLLY   *(Brightly)*   Okay, Evy.

EVY   And none of the Evy crap . . . I'm your mother. I want a little respect, for chrissakes!
(EVY starts to remove the tablecloth from the table as POLLY, beaming, exits into the kitchen)

Curtain

Act Two

It is three weeks later, about nine o'clock at night. POLLY *is thumbing through a private phone book. She finds a number and dials. She looks at her watch, concerned.*

POLLY *(Into the phone)* . . . Hello? . . . Is this Joe Allen's Bar? . . . Could you tell me if Evelyn Meara is there, please? . . . *Evy* Meara, that's right . . . I see . . . Was she there at all today? . . .
> *(The front door opens, unseen by* POLLY. EVY *enters carrying a Saks Fifth Avenue shopping bag)*

EVY   I'm here, I'm here. Just what I need, a trusting daughter.
> *(She closes the door)*

POLLY *(Into the phone)*   Never mind. Thank you.
> *(She hangs up and turns to* EVY. EVY *puts down the packages)*

EVY   If you knew what a terrific day I had you wouldn't be worrying about me . . . I've got sensational news . . . I was picked up today . . . He was eighty-six years old with a cane and a limp, but he really dug me. I don't think he could see me or hear me too good but we really hit it off . . . If I don't get any better offers this week, I'm going to contact him at the Home. Hello, pussycat, give your mother a kiss. *(She kisses* POLLY *on the cheek;* POLLY *receives it coldly)* What's wrong?

POLLY It's almost nine o'clock.

EVY You're kidding?

POLLY *(Points to the clock on the mantel)* I'm not kidding. It's almost nine o'clock.

EVY All right, don't get excited. What did I miss, the eclipse, what happened?

POLLY You don't call, you don't leave a note, you don't tell me where you're going to be. I'm expecting you home for dinner at six-thirty and you don't show and I'm scared to death. What happened? Where were you?

EVY Hanging around the men's room in the subway . . . I had a good day. You want to hear the details or you want to yell at me?

POLLY I want to yell at you.

EVY You can't yell at me, I'm your mother. I missed your dinner. Oh, God, Polly, I'm sorry. What did you make?

POLLY I don't know. Something out of the cookbook. It was brown and it was hot . . . If you want some, it's in the kitchen now. It's yellow and it's cold.

EVY *(Hugging her)* Don't be mad at me. All I've got in the world is you and that eighty-six-year-old gimp—don't be mad at me. Let me tell you what happened today.

POLLY Did you eat?

EVY Yes, I think so . . . Listen to what happened. I ran in-to this old girl friend of mine who used to work in the clubs—

POLLY   What do you mean, you think so? Don't you know if you ate or not?

EVY   I ate, I ate! I had a sandwich for lunch. I'll run up to Lenox Hill and take an x-ray for you . . . Will you listen to my story?

POLLY   You mean you haven't had anything to eat except lunch?

EVY   It didn't say "lunch" on the sandwich. Maybe it was a "dinner" sandwich, I don't know. What are you taking in school this week, nagging? Let me tell you my story.

POLLY   You don't sleep well and I never see you eat, so I'm worried about you.

EVY   Who says I don't sleep well?

POLLY   I watch you at night.

EVY   Then *you're* the one who doesn't sleep well.

POLLY   You're in the living room until five, six in the morning, pacing and smoking and coughing. I hear you in there.

EVY   It's the television. I listen to cancer commercials.

POLLY   Making phone calls in the middle of the night . . . Who were you calling at four o'clock in the morning?

EVY   The weather bureau.

POLLY   At four o'clock in the morning?

EVY   I like to know what it's going to be like at five o'clock . . . Jesus! Two more years of this, you're going to be a professional pain in the ass.

POLLY   Okay, fine with me. If you don't give a crap, I don't
give a crap.

EVY   And watch your goddamned language.

POLLY   If you don't watch yours, why should I watch
mine?

EVY   I talk this way. It's an impediment. You want me to
wear braces on my mouth?

POLLY   You might as well. You never *eat* anything except
a cup of coffee for breakfast.

EVY   What the hell difference does it make?

POLLY   Because if you don't take care of your body, it's not
going to take care of you.

EVY   I don't want to take care of my body. I want somebody
else to take care of it. Why do you think I'm talking to
eighty-year-old men?

POLLY   You're infuriating. It's like talking to a child.

EVY   *(Turns away)*   I don't get any respect. How the hell am
I going to be a mother if I don't get any respect?

POLLY   How am I going to respect you when you don't
respect yourself?

EVY   *(Looks up in despair)*   Oh, Christ, I'm a flop mother.
Three weeks and I blew it. Don't be angry, Polly. Don't
be mad at me.

POLLY   And stop apologizing. You're my mother. Make *me*
apologize to you for talking the way I did.

EVY   It won't happen again, sweetheart, I promise.

POLLY (*Vehemently*)   Don't promise *me*, promise yourself! I can't live my life *and* yours. *You've* got to take over, *you've* got to be the one in charge around here.

EVY   Listen, you're really getting me crazy now. Why don't you write all the rules and regulations nice and neat on a piece of paper and I'll do whatever it says. Put on one page where I yell at you, and one page where you yell at me . . . Now you want to hear what happened to me this afternoon or not?

POLLY (*It's hard not to like* EVY; POLLY *smiles at her*)   What happened this afternoon?

EVY   I think I have a job.

POLLY   You're kidding. Where?

EVY   Well . . . (*Pacing*) I was in Gucci's looking for a birth-day present for Toby . . . when suddenly I meet this old girl friend of mine who used to be a vocalist in this sing-ing group . . . Four Macks and a Truck or some god-damned thing . . . Anyway, she can't get over my gorgeous new figure and asks what I'm doing lately and I tell her . . . I'm looking for good honest work, preferably around a lot of single men, like an aircraft carrier, Okinawa, something like that . . . You're looking at me funny. If you're thinking of heating up the cold yellow stuff, forget it.

POLLY   I'm just listening.

EVY   All right . . . Well, she starts to tell me how she's out of the business now and is married to an Italian with four restaurants on Long Island and right away I dig he's in with the mob. I mean, one restaurant, you're in business;

four restaurants, it's the Mafia . . . Anyway, he's got a place in Garden City and he's looking for an attractive hostess who says, "Good evening, right this way please," and wriggles her behind and gets a hundred and ninety bucks a week . . . So I played it very cool, and nonchalantly got down on my knees, kissed her shoes, licked her ankles and carried her packages out the store.

POLLY   A hostess in a restaurant? Is that what you want to do?

EVY   No, what I *want* to do is be a masseur at the New York Athletic Club but there are no openings . . . Can I finish my story?

POLLY   Why don't you finish your story?

EVY   Thank you, I'll finish my story . . . So we go around the corner to Schrafft's and she buys me a sherry and we sit there chatting like a couple of Scarsdale debutantes— me, the former lush, and her, a chippie married to Joe Bananas . . . And she writes down the address and I have to be—*(Consults a scrap of paper from her pocket)*—at the Blue Cockatoo Restaurant in Garden City at ten o'clock tomorrow morning, where Lucky Luciano's nephew will interview me. All this in one day, *plus* getting my knees rubbed by an eighty-six-year-old degenerate on the crosstown bus . . . And you're going to sit there and tell me there's no God . . . *(She looks at* POLLY *expectantly, hoping* POLLY *will be as exuberant and enthusiastic about her prospects as she is. But* POLLY *just glares at her)* . . . What's the matter?

POLLY   You had a glass of sherry?

EVY   *(Turns away)*   Oh, Christ.

POLLY   Why did you have a glass of sherry?

EVY   Because the waitress put it down in front of me.

POLLY   They don't put it down in front of you unless you order it. I don't understand you.

EVY   I don't understand *you!* I rush home happy, excited, bubbling with good news and who do I find when I get here—a seventeen-year-old cop! I am not loaded, I am not smashed, I am thrilled to death because I spent a whole day out of this house and I came home alive and noticed and even wanted.

POLLY   Do you need a drink to feel that?

EVY   I was tense, I was afraid of blowing the job. So I had one stinking little drink. Did you ever have a cocktail in Schrafft's? Half of it is painted on the glass.

POLLY   That isn't the point. You could have had coffee or tea or milk.

EVY   Thank you, Miss, when do we land in Chicago? . . . I don't want to talk about it any more. Go inside and study. When you pass French, we'll discuss it in a foreign language. Until then, shape up or ship out or whatever the hell that expression is.

POLLY   *(A pause)*   No, listen *(Looks at her quietly a moment)* I think it's terrific.

EVY   You think what's terrific?

POLLY   About today, about getting the job. I really do. When will you start?

53

EVY   Well, in the first place, I didn't get it yet. And in the second place, I'm not so sure I'm going to take it.

POLLY *(Puzzled)*   Then what's all the excitement about?

EVY   About being asked . . . About being wanted.

POLLY   I'm sorry—I don't think I understand.

EVY *(Goes over to* POLLY *and holds her head in her arms)*   Please God, I hope you never do . . . *(Smiles at her, trying to be more cheerful)* Listen, how about one more chance at being a mother? If I screw up, you can buy out my contract for a hundred dollars and I'll move out.

POLLY *(Takes* EVY*'s hand)*   Who's going to bring me up?

EVY *(Shrugs)*   I'll set you on automatic . . . *(Crosses back to her shopping bag)* Hey, come on, get dressed. We have a party that started fifteen minutes ago.

POLLY   What party?

EVY   Toby's birthday. *(She takes a present from the shopping bag)* She's forty years old today. She's promised to take off her make-up and reveal her true identity.

POLLY   I've got to study. I have a science test on Monday.

EVY   Flunk it! Men don't like you if you're too smart. *(She takes out a bottle of champagne. She looks at* POLLY, *who stares at her meaningfully)* I'm pouring! That's all I'm doing is pouring.

POLLY   Who's coming?

EVY   Jimmy, Marty and Toby.
       *(*EVY *starts to cross to the kitchen with the champagne bottle, and* POLLY *starts for the bedroom)*

POLLY   What should I wear? How about the blue chif-
fon?

EVY   You can wear black crepe as long as your boobs don't
bounce around.
    (She moves toward the kitchen)

POLLY *(At the bedroom door)*   Mother?

EVY   Yes?

POLLY   Don't take that job. You're too good for it. Hold out
for something better.

EVY   I'm so glad you said that. Who the Christ even knows
where Garden City is? . . . Hey, let's have a good time
tonight. I'm beginning to feel like my old self again.

POLLY   Hey, listen, I forgot to tell you. We have a lunch
date tomorrow.

EVY *(In kitchen, busy with bottles)*   Who has a lunch date?

POLLY   We do. You, me and Daddy.
    (EVY *stops what she's doing and comes out to the kitchen*
    doorway)

EVY *(Dismayed)*   *What* Daddy?

POLLY   *My* Daddy. You remember, Felicia's husband?
. . . Twelve o'clock at Rumpelmayer's.

EVY   Why didn't you tell me?

POLLY   Because I never see you. *Now* I see you. He just
wants to have lunch with us, talk, see how we're getting
along.

EVY   We're getting along fine.

POLLY He knows. He just wants to see.

EVY You mean he's checking to see what shape I'm in?
Christ, he's going to look in my ears, under my finger-
nails—I'll never pass.

POLLY He just wants to talk.

EVY Is he gonna ask questions, like what's the capital of
Bulgaria?

POLLY Stop worrying. It'll be all right. I've got to get
dressed. Oh, and if he does, the capital is Sofia.
(She goes into the bedroom)

EVY *(Standing there a moment)* Just what I needed. A physi-
cal examination in Rumpelmayer's. *(Starts into the kitchen)*
I should have had *two* sherrys today.
(There is a moment's pause. The doorbell rings)

POLLY Are you getting it?

EVY *(Comes out of the kitchen)* If I was getting it I wouldn't
be looking for jobs all day . . . Get dressed. (EVY crosses
to the door and opens it. JIMMY *stands there, looking glum
and expressionless. He walks past her into the room.* EVY *closes
the door)* No kiss? . . . No hello? . . . Aren't you going
to look up, maybe you're in the wrong apartment? (JIM-
MY *sits without taking off his coat. He chews his thumbnail.
His leg begins to shake)* If you're that hungry, have some
nuts. *(He doesn't acknowledge)* What's the matter? What
happened?

JIMMY *(His leg is still shaking)* I'm okay, I'm not upset any
more, I'm all right . . . I know my leg is shaking but I'm
all right.

EVY   Why? What's wrong?

JIMMY   They pushed the opening of the show back one
night . . . It's opening Tuesday instead of Monday.

EVY   All right, it's Tuesday instead of Monday. What's so
terrible?

JIMMY   It's also another actor instead of me. They fired me.
The little son of a bitch fired me three nights before the
opening.

EVY   Oh, Christ.

JIMMY   Fired by a nineteen-year-old producer from Oklahoma A&M . . . Look at that leg. Do you realize the
tension that must be going on in my body right now?

EVY   Oh, Jimmy, no, don't tell me.

JIMMY   If he didn't like me, why'd he hire me in the first
place, heh? . . . The entire cast is shocked. Shocked, Evy.
Three nights before the opening.

EVY   They must be shocked.

JIMMY   He didn't even get somebody else to tell me. He
wanted to tell me himself . . . He stood there with a little
smile on his goddamned baby face and said, "Sorry,
Jimmy, it's just not working out." Nineteen years old,
can you imagine, Evy? . . . Ten thousand kids a month
getting drafted and they leave *this* one behind to produce
my show.

EVY   What can I say? What can I do?

JIMMY   Three nights before the opening. My name was in
the Sunday *Times* ad. I've got eighteen relatives from

Paterson, New Jersey, coming to the opening. Six of them already sent me telegrams . . . My Aunt Rosario sent me a Candygram. I already ate the goddamned candy.

EVY   Oh, God, I can't bear it. Tell me what to do for you.

JIMMY   Everybody in the cast wanted to walk out on the show. I wouldn't let them. Even the director was crazy about me . . . I can't breathe, I can't catch my breath, I'm so upset . . . I gotta calm down, Evy, I'll be all right.

EVY   I know how you feel. I swear. I know exactly how you feel.

JIMMY   You do? You know how it feels for a grown man to plead and beg to a child, Evy? A *child!* . . . I said to him, "You're not happy, I'll do it any way you want. Faster, slower, louder, I'll wear a dress, I'll shave my head, I'll relieve myself on the stage in front of my own family— I'm an actor, give me a chance to act." . . . He turned his back on me and shoved a Tootsie Roll in his mouth.

EVY   Listen, maybe the play won't be a hit. Maybe it'll be a bomb—it'll close in one night. You're lucky you're out of it.

JIMMY   What do you mean, maybe? It's got no chance. It's the worst piece of crap ever put on a stage. That's why I'm so humiliated. To get fired from a piece of garbage like that, who's gonna want me for something good?

EVY   *(Puts her arm around him)*   Screw him, sweetheart, you don't need them. *(She hugs him)* Something better'll come along.

JIMMY   When? Next Christmas at Korvette's? *(He pulls away from her)* Do you know who they gave my part to?

The understudy. He's not even a full-time actor, he drives a cab in the day . . . A Puerto Rican cabdriver. Can't speak English. He got me coffee the first two weeks, now he's got my part . . . Look how my neck is throbbing. That's blood pumping into the brain, I'm going to have a hemorrhage.

EVY   You're not going to have a hemorrhage.

JIMMY   What am I going to tell my family in Jersey? My sister's taking my twelve-year-old niece, her first time in the theater, never saw me on the stage, she's gonna think she's got a Puerto Rican uncle . . . I was thinking maybe I wouldn't tell anyone. Opening night I'll show up in the theater, walk out on the stage. Two of us will play the same part, one in Spanish, one in English—the critics will love it.

EVY   Whatever you say. You want the theater blown up, the kid rubbed out—I'm in with the Mafia, they'd be glad to do it. (JIMMY *still has not removed his sheepskin coat*) . . . But I don't want you upset, not tonight. It's Toby's birthday, I'm counting on you for laughs.

JIMMY   (*Looks at his hand*)   Look at my fingers. There's no color in the nails. That's a hemorrhage. I'm having a goddamned hemorrhage and I can't find it.

EVY   (*Crosses to him, tries to take his coat off*)   Give me your coat. Come on, give me your coat, for chrissakes, you wanna catch pneumonia?

JIMMY   What the hell difference does it make?
(*But* JIMMY *suddenly buries his face in his hands and begins to sob, deeply and uncontrollably*)

59

EVY *(Almost withers at the sight)* Oh, God, Jimmy, no, don't. *(She wrings her hands helplessly)* Jimmy, listen, you can't do this to me . . . Stop it, Jimmy, you hear? I won't stand for it.

JIMMY *(Sobbing)* What the hell am I going to do?

EVY You're not going to crack up on me. I'm not going to get stuck with a dud party. Come on, Jimmy . . .

JIMMY *(Still sobbing)* Who am I kidding, Evy? I'm not going to make it, I'm *never* going to make it in this business.

EVY Go ahead. You want to destroy me? You want to tear my guts out? You know I can't handle it.

JIMMY Twenty-two years and I'm still expecting to get discovered. The oldest goddamned newcomer in show business.

EVY *(Near tears)* Listen, you bastard, if *I* start to cry, it's all over. You really want to see crying? I'll make you look foolish.

JIMMY I should have stayed at Bonwit's. I'd have been a floorwalker today.

EVY No you wouldn't, because you're going to become a star. A great big star! You're already a shitheel—there's no point in wasting it.

JIMMY *(Grabs* EVY *and clings to her)* Don't say anything. Don't say anything to Toby.

EVY I won't. I promise. Not a word.

JIMMY Evy, you've seen me on the stage. You know I can be good. Was I good, Evy? Tell me—I really have to know.

EVY You're the best. There's no one better. You ring a doorbell, the house comes down . . . Let me get you a drink. You'll feel much better if you have a drink.

JIMMY I'm not Olivier. I never said I was Olivier, did I?

EVY I don't even like Olivier. I can't understand him half the time.
     (She goes into the kitchen)

JIMMY *(Talking into the kitchen)* Remember *Mr. Roberts* at Bucks County? Or *Born Yesterday* in Westport? I never heard laughs like that in my life . . . Did you? The truth! Did you?

EVY *(Offstage)* I have never heard laughs like that in my life.

JIMMY In my life, I never heard laughs like that . . . And I don't have to get laughs all the time. My God, the things I've done . . . *Phaedra, Mother Courage, Rhinoceros, The Balcony, Detective Story* . . . Jesus, remember *Detective Story?* The second hood? I was incredible.

EVY *(Offstage)* You were brilliant.
     (We hear a cork pop from a champagne bottle)

JIMMY When did you see me in *Detective Story?* I did that in Columbus, Ohio.

EVY *(Comes out with the champagne bottle and two glasses)* You were so brilliant I didn't have to see it.
(She hands JIMMY *a glass. He takes it without being aware he has it)*

JIMMY I played the Dauphin in *St. Joan* at the Cleveland Auditorium three years before that nineteen-year-old rich Oklahoma idiot schmuck was born.
*(*EVY *pours champagne into his glass, then hers)*

EVY *(Takes a sip)* Forget it. He's not worth it.

JIMMY I actually pleaded with him. I humiliated myself in front of the entire cast. I had no shame. No shame, Evy. *(He drinks)* Opening night my mother will throw herself in front of a rented limousine.

EVY That's the best thing that could happen to *your* mother.
(She sips a little more)

JIMMY I don't wish anybody in the world harm. I don't curse anybody. I want everybody to live their lives healthy and without pain . . . But I pray that little bastard gets a Baby Ruth stuck in his throat and chokes him on the spot. *(He drinks more champagne.* EVY *pours more into his glass. He suddenly watches her and realizes what's happening)* Oh, my God, what am I doing? I'm sitting here drinking with you. Are you crazy? Are you out of your mind? Put that glass down.
(He reaches for it, but she pulls it away)

EVY I'm not drinking, I'm sipping.

JIMMY You've already sipped a whole glass. Give it to me.

Maureen Stapleton as EVY MEARA *&* Charles Siebert *as* LOU TANNER.

EVY   You think I'm going to stand here and watch you have a breakdown on ginger ale? I need help too.

JIMMY   You put your lips to that glass one more time, you're going to need more than help.

EVY   (*Holds the glass up*)   All right, I'm through, I'm through. (*Then she raises the glass to her lips and finishes it*) There! All right?

JIMMY   Why do you do that to me? Didn't I have enough heartache today?

EVY   A grown man is crying, you want me to sit down and read *Newsweek?* I'm sorry, I panicked.

JIMMY   You didn't panic, you drank. Panicking is when you scream and run around like a lunatic.

EVY   I will. I promise. Next time I'll panic. Better still, don't tell me your problems. You got a twelve-year-old niece, tell her your troubles. Kids love to cry.

JIMMY   (*Turns away from her*)   I'm standing there drinking with her. I see the glass in her hand and I'm drinking with her.

EVY (*Walks around in front of him to get his attention*)   Don't be mad at me. Everybody's mad at me today. Show me a little tenderness, I'll show you a terrific person.

JIMMY   (*Looks at her; he wilts*)   How could I be mad at you? You loved me in *Detective Story* and never even saw it.
    (*He hugs her. The doorbell rings*)

EVY   (*In a low voice*)   Don't tell Polly. Don't tell her I drank, tell her I panicked.

JIMMY   Some mood I'm in for a party. Christ!

EVY *(Calls out)*   Hey, Pol, come on, they're here.

POLLY *(Offstage)*   I don't know how to work the brassière.

EVY *(At the door; to* JIMMY*)*   Try and be happy tonight. You won't have to do it for another year. (JIMMY *nods cheerlessly at her. She opens the door.* TOBY *stands there, looking absolutely ravishing in a new dress. She smiles at* EVY) Oh, God, that's a pretty woman. Look, Jimmy. Look at the pretty woman.

JIMMY *(Smiles)*   Oh, yes. That's a pretty woman.

EVY *(To* JIMMY*)*   Go, sweetheart. Go kiss the pretty woman. (JIMMY *crosses in front of* EVY *and kisses* TOBY *on the cheek)*

JIMMY   Happy birthday, darling.

TOBY *(Smiles)*   Thank you.
(*She speaks softly.* EVY *crosses to* TOBY)

EVY   Happy birthday, pretty woman. (*She hugs* TOBY)

TOBY   Thank you, Evelyn.
(*She goes to the sofa and sits down, opening her purse)*

EVY *(Looks toward the outside hall)*   Isn't Marty with you?

TOBY   No.
(JIMMY *closes the door)*

EVY   Is he coming later?

TOBY *(Busy powdering)*   I don't think so.

EVY *(Looks at* JIMMY, *then at* TOBY*)*   You don't *think* so? Don't you know?

TOBY Yes, I know. He's not coming later. *(Looks around)* Isn't Polly here?

EVY He's not coming for your birthday party? . . . Are you going to tell me he's *working* tonight?

TOBY No, he's not working. He just couldn't come. To my birthday party.
> *(She takes out the powder puff again and begins to powder her already highly powdered face)*

EVY Why not?

TOBY Well, I didn't catch everything he said . . . because he was very busy packing . . . but it seems that Martin wants a divorce. *(She smiles at them as though she has told them nothing more startling than "it's raining outside." JIMMY and EVY stare at her, stunned. TOBY suddenly controls the flood of tears that are threatening to come by patting her hand to her eye, but we do hear a faint sigh from her)* Is there anything to eat in the refrigerator?
> *(She gets up and quickly crosses into the kitchen to release the floodgates)*

JIMMY *(Looks up to heaven, clasping his hands)* Oh, sweet Mother of Jesus! You just going to stand there? Say something to her? Do something. *(But EVY stands there)* Toby! Toby!
> *(He runs off to the kitchen after TOBY. EVY turns, looks around, sees that no one is looking and quickly pours herself a glass of champagne. She drinks it quickly, then puts the glass down. POLLY emerges from the bedroom, looking lovely and feminine)*

POLLY *(Arms extended)* Happy birthday! *(Looks around)* Where's the birthday lady?

EVY *(Motions toward the kitchen)* With the great American actor.

POLLY Do I look all right?

EVY *(Despondent)* Don't count on applause.
(JIMMY *comes out of the kitchen*)

JIMMY She's all right. Give her a couple of seconds. (*To* POLLY) Hello, Angel. Don't you look gorgeous.

POLLY *(Beaming)* I was thinking of wearing this for your opening. Okay? (JIMMY *looks at* EVY, *then crosses away.* POLLY *looks at them, then to* EVY) I detect tenseness. Is there tenseness at this party?

EVY And it's only ten after nine.
(TOBY *comes out of the kitchen. She seems composed*)

TOBY I love the cake, Evy. It's a beautiful cake . . . Oh, Polly, how sweet. How sweet and beautiful you are. I was the same way.

POLLY *(Goes to her)* Happy birthday, Toby.
(They kiss)

TOBY Thank you, darling. It's so good to see you. I never see you. I was so anxious to see you tonight and spend some time with you. I never spend enough time with you. Would you excuse us, darling, I have to talk to your mother.

POLLY *(Puzzled)* Now?

EVY Now.

POLLY *(Shrugs)* I'll study French. Call me when the games begin. *(She goes into the bedroom)*

TOBY   She's going to be beautiful, Evy. There is nothing so important in a woman's life as being beautiful . . . *(There is a pause. No one says anything)* Anyone want to hear about my divorce?

JIMMY   You're not serious. You had a fight. That's all it was, a little fight, right?

TOBY   No, there's going to be an actual divorce. He is, at the very moment we're speaking, getting advice from his brother, the lawyer, and sympathy from his understanding sister-in-law who happens to know a great deal about sympathy because of those two huge warts on the side of her nose . . . I'm fine. I'm perfectly fine. Really.

EVY   What happened tonight? Don't describe what you were wearing, just the details.

TOBY   There are no details. He wants a divorce, it's that simple . . . Do you have any canapés, darling, I think I forgot to eat in all the excitement.

EVY   You caught him at the Americana Hotel with a stewardess from Delta Airlines, right?

TOBY   It wouldn't bother me if I caught him at his brother's house with his sister-in-law . . . Or his sister's house with his brother-in-law . . . It's not another woman.

JIMMY   Then what is it?

TOBY   I must have something to drink.

EVY   *(To JIMMY)*   The ladies need a drink.

JIMMY   *(Quickly)*   *I'll* get it.
(*He moves hurriedly and gets the champagne bottle from where* EVY *left it, and pours a glass for* TOBY)

TOBY *(Takes a deep breath)* Martin—has grown accustomed to my face. *(She is visibly wounded but is trying hard not to show the hurt)* Accustomed to my touch, accustomed to my voice . . . and I think he's a little bored with my hair. *(She looks at them, forces a smile, sips a little wine)* He's devoted to me . . . He is respectful of me . . . He is indebted to me . . . but he's having a lot of trouble sleeping with me. For some inexplicable reason—"inexplicable" is his word— he has had no desire to make sexual advances towards me. He makes them, but there's no desire. It's as though someone were in back of him "pushing" . . . He is not tired . . . He is not overworked . . . He is not distracted . . . He is simply—"turned off." That's *my* word.

JIMMY *(About to say something helpful)* Toby, for God's sakes—

TOBY Did you know . . . that in 1950 I was voted the prettiest girl at the University of Michigan? . . . An All-American halfback was willing to give up a trip to the Rose Bowl for one night of my favors . . . In 1951 I switched schools and was voted the prettiest girl at the University of Southern California . . . I received, on the average, fifteen sexual proposals a week—at least two from the faculty—

EVY All right, Toby—

TOBY When I was sixteen I was offered a seven-year contract by RKO Pictures. They knew I couldn't act; they didn't even care. They said the way I looked, it wasn't important . . . When I was seventeen years old, a married psychiatrist in Los Angeles drove his car into a tree because I wouldn't answer his phone calls. You can read all of this in my diaries, I still have them.

EVY   Toby, please stop.

TOBY   When I was nineteen I had an affair with a boy who
was the son of the largest book publisher in the world
. . . When I was twenty, I had an affair *with* the largest
book publisher in the world . . . The son threatened to kill
the father but by then I was having an affair with the
youngest symphony conductor in the world.

EVY   Jimmy, for God's sakes, will you say something to
her?

TOBY *(Accelerating)*   When I was twenty-three, I *slept* with
a member of the British Royal Household. I slept with
him. In the British Royal House . . . There is a Senator
living in Washington, D.C., today who will vote any way
I want him to vote by my spending just one morning in
Washington, D.C. . . . I have had more men—men in
politics, in the arts, in the sciences, more of the most
influential men in the world—in love with me, desirous
of me, *hungry* for me, than any woman I ever met in my
entire life . . . And that son-of-a-bitch four-hundred-dol-
lar-a-week television salesman tells me *he isn't interested?*
. . . *Then let him get out, I don't need him! (And she begins to
sob uncontrollably)* Evy . . . Evy!
    (EVY, *of course, is distraught with her own inability to
    help*)

EVY *(Paces)*   Jimmy, do something or I'll kill myself.
    (JIMMY *quickly crosses to* TOBY *and sits on the arm of her
    chair, putting his arm around her to comfort her*)

JIMMY   It's all right, Toby, it's all right.

TOBY *(Looks up at* JIMMY)   I am still beautiful and I am still
desirable, I don't care how old I am.

JIMMY   Of course you are, my God! . . . Evy, give her some more wine.

TOBY (*To* EVY)   Evy, no woman has ever taken care of herself the way I have. (EVY *goes to the champagne bottle*) I am forty years old today, and my skin is as smooth and as creamy white as it was when I was sixteen.
(EVY *hands* JIMMY *a glass of champagne*)

JIMMY (*Giving the glass to* TOBY)   Drink this. Come on, Toby, you'll feel better.

TOBY   We spent two months on the beach at Westhampton last summer, and the sun never once touched my body . . . I wore more clothes on the beach than I do in New York in January . . . In Acapulco last year the Mexicans thought I was some kind of a White Goddess. They would bow to me on the streets. Jimmy, remember I told you that story?

JIMMY   I remember that story.

TOBY (*Addressing* EVY *again*)   Last December in Los Angeles, that boy I had an affair with, the book publisher's son, called me at the Beverly Hills Hotel, *dying* to see me. He came over and we had cocktails in the Polo Lounge . . . He looked like my father. My *father*, Evy . . . And then the waiter came over and, I swear—may God strike me dead as I sit here with my dearest friends—the waiter asked for my I.D. card . . . I don't even think it's twenty-one in California, I think you have to be eighteen. I know it's dark in the Polo Lounge, but it's not *that* dark.

JIMMY (*To* EVY, *as though it would help* TOBY)   It's not, I've been there, I know.

TOBY *(Sips a little more champagne)* I'm not a stupid woman, I know that. I've traveled a lot, I'm well-read, well-educated, I went to two universities. I have had marvelous intellectual conversations with some of the most brilliant men in the world . . . but the thing that men admire most in a woman is her femininity and her beauty . . . That's the truth, Evy, I know it is. *(To* JIMMY*)* Isn't that the first thing you men look for in a woman, Jimmy?

JIMMY *(Hesitates)* Yes, I suppose it is.

TOBY *(Back to* EVY*)* I know I'm vain, Evy. I never pretended I'm not. I devote my whole day to myself, to my face, to my body . . . I sleep all morning so my eyes won't be red. I bathe twice a day in soft water. I buy the world's most expensive creams. I have a Japanese man who lives in White Plains come down twice a week just to do my feet. Did you know that, Evy? *(*EVY *nods.* TOBY *turns to* JIMMY*)* Did you?

JIMMY I didn't know he was Japanese.

TOBY I swear. He says I have the feet of an Oriental woman. Can you imagine, Evy. Born in Grand Rapids, Michigan, with the feet of an Oriental woman . . . But I've never done it for *me*. None of it . . . It's what Martin wanted when he came into his house at night, what all men want—femininity and beauty . . . But Evy, if it no longer interests Martin, then I assure you . . . somewhere, soon, someplace, someone else will be very . . . very . . . very . . . interested!
    (Her voice has trailed off, becoming almost inaudible at the end. There is a long, desperate silence in the room)

EVY *(Finally)* For purely medicinal purposes, I'm having a drink.
> *(She starts for the bottle)*

JIMMY *(Warning)* Evy!

EVY I'm only a hundred and thirty pounds but if you try and stop me, I'll kill you . . . *One* drink, for chrissakes.

JIMMY You *had* one drink.

EVY For *your* story. Now I need one for hers.
> *(She pours a drink)*

TOBY *(Looks up as if in the room for the first time)* What's the matter? What's going on?

EVY *Nothing's* going on, but it's going to start right now . . . We've *all* had a few minor setbacks, but it's a birthday party—and I don't give a crap if the room is on fire, we're going to start having some fun. *(She drinks quickly from her wine glass, then looks at the bottle and holds it up)* We need a new bottle. *(Calls out)* Polly! Fun and games.

TOBY *(Pulling her things together)* I'm not staying, I just wanted to talk to someone.

EVY Nobody's leaving this room until we're all happy. Now sit down, dammit. Drink your booze. *(She drinks a little more from her glass. The wine is now beginning to take effect on* EVY; *since she is an alcoholic, it doesn't take much wine or time)* Jesus, what a bunch of depressing people.
> *(*POLLY *comes out)*

POLLY *(With a big smile)* Okay, who do I dance with?

EVY *(Points to* POLLY*)* Now *that's* the kind of person you invite to a party. *(To* POLLY*)* So far it's just you and me, kid, but we're gonna goose things up. Put on one of your records. I'll get some more wine. *(Starts for the kitchen)* And none of that folk-singing crap where they throw babies in the Talahachee River. I want some real music, pussycat.

> *(She goes off into the kitchen)*

POLLY *(Looks after her)*   Is she all right? What's going on?

JIMMY   Nothing. Everything's fine.

TOBY   I think I must have upset her. Did I upset her, Jimmy?

JIMMY   It's not you, it's everybody. We're all upsetting each other. Some friends . . .

POLLY   She had a drink at Schrafft's this afternoon, did she tell you?

JIMMY   At Schrafft's? Who the hell goes off the wagon at Schrafft's?

TOBY   I shouldn't have said all that to her. I could see she was very upset.

> *(They both look worriedly toward* EVY *in the kitchen . . . A cork explodes.* EVY *comes out with an opened bottle of champagne)*

EVY   Goddamned cheap champagne—I had to make the noise with my tongue. Glasses up, everyone. *(She looks at the silent phonograph, then at* POLLY) You're not going to play that louder, right?

POLLY *(Going for the bottle)*   Let me pour it, Mother.

EVY   Ooh, you hear that? Mother, she calls me. If it's one thing I know how to get, it's respect.

7 5

TOBY Evy, don't pay attention to what I said before. Everything's going to be all right, honestly.

EVY (*To* TOBY) No, listen, you have a major problem. You and Marty are only making it two times a day, if I were you, I'd kill myself.
(*She pours wine into* TOBY'S *glass*)

TOBY (*Embarrassed*) Evy, please. Can we discuss this later?

EVY What's the matter? You're worried about Polly? *My* Polly? You don't know about kids today, do you? (*She puts her arm around* POLLY) She could give you a sex lecture right now, your eyebrows would fall out. (*To* POLLY) Am I right? Is that the truth, Polly?
(POLLY *forces a smile and shrugs*)

JIMMY May I have the wine, please?

EVY What do you think, kids learn about sex today the way you and I did? In rumble seats? They have closed-circuit television—(*To* POLLY) Am I right? Actual demonstrations. Two substitute teachers go at it in the gymnasium and the kids take notes. Is that the truth?

POLLY (*Smiles, embarrassed*) That's the truth.

EVY It's the truth. Polly has a sixteen-year-old girl friend in school who got knocked up for homework. Am I lying? Heh?

POLLY (*Weakly*) Nope.

EVY (EVY *pours some wine into her own glass and drinks it. She laughs*) Oh, Christ, that's funny. (*No one else laughs*) Look how funny you all think it is . . . Gee, what a terrific party.

Later on we'll get some fluid and embalm each other. Polly, get a glass. You have to drink to Toby's birthday.

POLLY *(Reaches for the bottle)*   Can I pour it myself?

EVY *(Holding back the bottle)*   What's the matter, you don't trust me? One glass, that's all I'm going to have . . . My daughter is worried about me. *(She puts her arm around POLLY again)* Do you know what it is to have a daughter worried about you? It is the *single greatest* pleasure in the world . . . In the *world* . . . *(To TOBY)* You can have your toes tickled by a Jap—I'll take a daughter worrying about me any time. *(She sips from her glass. She is beginning to lose coordination and control)* I don't even deserve it. The truth, Polly, I don't deserve it. You grew up, you saw the bus driver more than you saw me, am I right?

JIMMY   Polly, why don't you get the cake?

EVY   No, it's all right, Polly and I understand each other. We have an agreement. She doesn't bug me about the past and I don't bug her about not wearing underwear.

TOBY   Evy, stop, you're embarrassing her.

EVY   I am not. Am I embarrassing you, sweetheart? I'm not embarrassing you, am I?

POLLY *(Good-naturedly)*   I'll let you embarrass me if you let me take your glass.

EVY *(Holds the glass away from POLLY but ignores her remark)* I told you I'm not embarrassing her. I mean the girl is *beautiful*. Toby, if you saw her sleeping in the raw you'd kill yourself. It's all firm. Remember "firm"? . . . You don't remember firm.

POLLY *(Forcing a smile)*   Okay, *now* I'm getting embarrassed.

77

EVY *(Going right on)*   The body of a young woman is God's greatest achievement . . . Of course, He could have built it to last longer, but you can't have everything.

TOBY   Evy, it's my birthday and you're not making me very happy. Let's not have any more wine.

EVY   Why doesn't everybody relax? It's like a goddamn telethon for palsy. Come on, a toast. A toast for my friend Toby. Jimmy, you do it. You're the toastmaster . . . A toast, everyone.

JIMMY   Evy, I don't think anyone's in the mood.

EVY   Well, *put* 'em in the mood. What else you got to do? You're not working!
(She pulls the reluctant JIMMY *to the middle of the floor)*

JIMMY   I'm never good at these things. I never know what to say.

EVY   Glasses up, everyone.
(She stands next to POLLY. EVY *seems to be unaware of the tension she is causing in the room. Once on alcohol, she enters a world of her own)*

JIMMY *(Holds up his glass)*   To Toby . . . whom we all love and cherish. Happy birthday.

POLLY   Happy birthday, Toby.
(They all drink)

TOBY   Thank you.

EVY   That's the toast? Sounds like she died of leukemia. "Fifty dollars donation in memory of Toby Landau, who

we loved and cherished . . ." She's alive, for chrissakes—
tell her what a great broad she is.

TOBY   It was a lovely toast, Evy . . . and I'm very touched.

EVY   You're a great broad, Toby. I want you to know it.
Only one who came to see me in the hospital. I'll never
forget you for that—

TOBY   Evy, stop, I'm going to cry again.

EVY   I don't care if you whistle Dixie through your ass, I'm
telling you I love you . . . (TOBY *looks at* POLLY) Whoops,
sorry, Polly. Mother's being naughty.
(She pours some more wine into her glass)

JIMMY   Evy, will you give me that bottle?

EVY   When it's empty, pussycat.

POLLY   Mother, should I get the cake now?

EVY   I'll *tell* you when to get the cake. I'm not ready for the
cake yet. What the hell's the big rush with the cake? I
didn't rent it, I bought it outright . . . I'm still telling
Toby how much I love her. *(She points to* TOBY *with the hand
holding the glass. The wine spills on* TOBY*'s dress)* Oh, Christ,
Jesus, I'm sorry . . . *(Tries wiping it with her hand)* On your
birthday, got you right in the crotch . . . Polly, get me a
Kleenex or something.

TOBY   It's all right, it'll dry.

EVY   It's ruined. Your two-hundred-and-fifty-dollar dress
is ruined . . . Listen, I want you to take my mink coat. I
paid thirty-two hundred bucks for it in 1941. You can get

about four dollars for it now and I'll pay you a little bit each week.

(*She's still rubbing* TOBY*'s dress*)

TOBY   Evy, it's all right, it's an old dress.

EVY   No kidding? I'll buy it from you. What do you want, about twenty dollars? I mean, it's not worth more, it's got a goddamned wine stain right in the front.

JIMMY   Polly, why don't you get the cake?

EVY (*Screams*)   Don't you touch that cake! I'm emceeing this party—

TOBY   Evy, please don't drink any more.

JIMMY   Evy, I'm asking you nicely for the last time. Put down the wine.

EVY   I am. I'm putting it down as fast as I can. (*She crosses to* TOBY) Listen, I got a first-class idea. Why don't you two move in with us? We don't need anybody else . . . Just us four girls. What do you say?

TOBY (*About to fall apart*)   Evy, I've got to go. (*Crossing the room*) Thank you for the party.

EVY   What party? Two salted peanuts, everyone took turns crying, and you fink out on me.

TOBY   Evy, I can't sit here and watch what's happening. (*At the door*) Polly, take care of her. I'll call you in the morning . . . (*To* EVY) Evy—I'm sorry if I did this to you.

(*She can't say any more; she turns and runs out*)

EVY (*Calls out*)   Wait a minute. Your present. I didn't give you your present. Polly, get her back.

POLLY She's gone, Mother.

EVY (*Playfully goes to* JIMMY) I believe this is your dance, Colonel Sanders, and by the way, I love your finger-lickin' chicken.

JIMMY Evy, Evy, you stupid bitch.

EVY Hey, hey, watch that kind of talk. I have a daughter here someplace.

JIMMY Then why do you act this way in front of her?

POLLY Jimmy, it's all right.

JIMMY It's *not* all right. She's drunk and disgusting and she doesn't give a damn about herself or anyone else. Well, then damn it, neither do I. Go on. Finish the bottle. Finish the whole goddamn case, for all I care.

EVY Okay, buster, you just talked yourself out of an opening-night party.

JIMMY And you just drank yourself out of a couple of friends. I don't want to see you any more, Evy. I swear to God. I am through. Finished forever, I've *had* it . . . Goodbye, Polly, I'm sorry.
     (*He goes quickly to the door*)

EVY How about a little kiss goodbye? (*She grabs his arm*) Come on, one little kiss on the lips. It'll make all the New York papers.

JIMMY Let go of me, damn it!
     (*He wrenches from* EVY *and runs out, leaving the door open.* EVY *rushes to the door and yells out*)

EVY (*Pleading*) Jimmy! Jimmy, come back, I'm sorry . . . Jimmy, don't leave me, you're the only man in my life.

(*But he's gone. She comes back into the apartment.* EVY *tries to compose herself in front of* POLLY) I guess this would be a good time to get the cake.

POLLY   I'm not hungry. I've got homework to do. I'll clean up later.

EVY   Oh, you're mad at me. I don't know what I did, but you're mad at me, right?

POLLY   I'm not mad at you, Mother.

EVY   What then? You're ashamed? Ashamed of your sweet little old mother because she had two tiny glasses of domestic wine?

POLLY   I'm not ashamed.

EVY   *Then what are you?*

POLLY   I'm sorry . . . I'm just plain sorry.
(*She looks at* EVY, *then slowly goes into the bedroom and closes the door behind her.* EVY *stands there*)

EVY *(Loudly)*   Sorry for what? For me? Well, don't be sorry for me because I don't need your goddamned teen-age pity . . . I'm terrific, baby, haven't you noticed? Cost me twenty-seven hundred bucks and I'm skinny and terrific and I can have any dirty old man in the neighborhood . . . *(Suddenly softening)* Oh, Jesus, Polly, I'm sorry *(Crosses to the bedroom door)* Polly, don't be mad . . . Come on out. We'll have our own private party . . . Look! Look, I'm gonna put on some music. *(Goes to the record player)* I've just had a request to play one of my old numbers. *(Takes out her album)* Come listen to mother sing when she was a big star, darling. *(Puts the record on the machine)* Well, not exactly a big star . . . But I once had a sandwich named after me at the Stage Delicatessen . . . *(The music starts. We hear* EVY *singing. She stands there listening, drinking from the wine glass)* That's not bad, is it? It's not bad . . . It's not *thrilling* but it's not bad. *(She sings along, looking around the room)* This is about the same size audiences I used to get. *(She crosses to the bedroom door)* Polly, please come out . . . I don't want to listen to me all by myself . . . Polly? *(No answer. She looks at the phone)* I am *not* going to listen all by myself . . . *(She crosses to phone, takes a deep breath and dials. Into the phone)* . . . Hello? Lou? . . . You alone? . . . Guess who wants to come over to your place?

Curtain

Act Three

It is the following morning, Saturday, about eleven o'clock.
POLLY *is seated on the piano bench, staring aimlessly and worriedly.*
TOBY, *in a polo coat over pajamas, sits on a chair, nervously smoking.*

TOBY   I'm not worried.

POLLY   You've told me that since eight o'clock this morning, Toby.

TOBY   *(Puffs again)*   She's all right. She's done this before. I am not worried.

POLLY   Is that why you've had nine cigarettes since you got here?

TOBY   I have other problems on my mind besides your mother's disappearance. *(Puffs)* If I get nicotine stains on my teeth, I'll never forgive her.

POLLY   She just walks out and disappears all night without saying a word. Where the hell could she be?

TOBY   Don't swear, darling, your mother wouldn't like it . . . You really should get some sleep, angel. You're going to get little ugly puffy rings under your eyes.

POLLY   I'm sorry, Toby. I've never gone through this before.

TOBY   She's put me through it for twelve years. That's why I wear such heavy make-up. Underneath this is my mother.

POLLY *(Determined)*   I'm not going to forgive her, Toby, I swear . . . The minute I hear she's all right, I'm not going to forgive her.
>   *(She starts to cry, rushes into the bedroom and closes the door behind her.* TOBY *picks up her coffee cup and starts to go into the kitchen, when the door opens. It's* EVY, *hiding her face)*

TOBY   Well, good morning.

EVY   That's entirely possible.

TOBY   Do you know what time it is?

EVY   November?

TOBY   Evy!

EVY   Later, Toby. I have to go to the john.

TOBY   I refuse to talk to your unbrushed hair all morning. Turn around and look at me. (EVY *turns around, revealing a black-and-blue eye*) Oh, God—your eye! Evy, what have you done?

EVY   You want to be my friend, Toby? No questions and no sympathy. I'm all right.

TOBY   I don't think I *want* to hear about it.

EVY   Where's Polly?

TOBY   She's been up all night calling everyone. I made her go in and lie down.

EVY   Well, if she sleeps for three weeks I may get away with it.

TOBY   You don't seem to be acting much like a woman who just got beaten up.

EVY   I didn't get beaten, Toby, just punched. One clean little punch, I never even felt it.

TOBY   Really? Have you seen what you look like?

EVY   Compared to you, what difference does it make? . . . I'm all right, I promise you.

TOBY   Sit down. Let me put some ice on it.

EVY   I've already had medical attention. A dog licked my face while I was down.

TOBY   Who did it?

EVY   What difference does it make?

TOBY   Because I feel responsible.

EVY   Come on, Toby. I got what I asked for last night because I wasn't getting anything else. *(She sits)* All right, I'm sitting. Are you happy now?

TOBY   How can I be happy when your face is half smashed in? How many places did you have to go before you found what you were looking for?

EVY   Just one. If there's one thing I know how to do, it's shop.

TOBY   *(Turns away)*   Oh, Christ, Evy, sometimes you disgust me.

EVY   That seems to be the general feeling around town.

TOBY   It was Lou Tanner, wasn't it?

EVY That's him. The man I love.

TOBY Jesus, I knew it. There was always something about
him that frightened me. You could see it in his eyes.

EVY Never mind the eyes, it's the big fist you gotta watch
. . . I wouldn't hate you if you left me alone now, Toby.

TOBY Why did you go there, Evy?

EVY He plays requests—I was lonesome.

TOBY Why did you start drinking yesterday? Everything
was going so good for you. Why, Evy?

EVY What do you want, a nice simple answer? When I was
six years old my father didn't take me to the circus . . .
How the hell do I know why I do anything?

TOBY Didn't you learn anything in ten weeks at the hospital?

EVY The doctor tried to explain, but I was too busy making a pass at him . . . If I knew, Toby, would it make any
difference?

TOBY It would help.

EVY If you haven't eaten in three months you don't want
a description of food, you want a little hot something in
the plate.

TOBY And did you get your fill last night, Evy? Did you get
your little hot something in the plate?

EVY No, but we negotiated for a while . . .

TOBY With someone like that? A deadbeat musician who
doesn't give a damn about hitting some drunken woman.

EVY You just don't get hit like that, you gotta ask for it
. . . I happened to make a bad choice. I broke his guitar.
I smashed it against the refrigerator, handed him the
pieces and said, "Now you can look for work you're
equipped to do." I thought it was cute. The man has no
sense of humor.

TOBY The truth, Evy. When he was beating you, did you
enjoy it?

EVY Well, for a second there I said to myself, it hurts like
hell—but it sure beats indifference. *(She gets up)* Is there
anything in the kitchen? I'm always hungry after a fight.

TOBY *(Angrily)* What fight? There was no fight. You just
stood there and let him beat the crap out of you.

EVY That's right, pussycat.

TOBY The way you let *everybody* beat the crap out of
you.

EVY Same as you. Only Marty doesn't punch, he just walks
out on you. In your own adorable way, you're no better
off than I am.

TOBY *(Still angry)* At least my face isn't beaten to a pulp.

EVY Terrific. You spent forty years being gorgeous and all
you've got to show for it is a turned-up little nose . . . We
cried for you yesterday; today is my turn.

TOBY At least I've *tried* to make things work. I've at least
made the *effort*.

EVY The only effort you make is opening your compact. If
you powdered Marty once in a while instead of your face,
you'd be wearing *his* pajamas now instead of yours.

TOBY   I powdered my goddamned face because I was afraid every time Marty looked at me too closely. Afraid he'd see what I was becoming.

EVY   Terriffic. Why don't you spend the rest of your life in the Beverly Hills Polo Lounge? You can put on a Shirley Temple dress and suck a lollipop . . . And next year you'll have an affair with the book publisher's grandson . . .

TOBY   Go to hell.

EVY   Toby, you know I love you. We're the same kind of broads. We both manage to screw up everything . . . The only difference is, you dress better doing it.

TOBY   Damn you, Evy. Damn you for being so goddamned honest all the time. Who needs the truth if this is what it gets you?

EVY   Listen, I'm willing to live a lie. As far as I'm concerned, I'm twenty-two with a cute little behind. Now find me a fellow who believes it.

TOBY   You're not twenty-two, you're forty-three. And you're an alcoholic with no sense of morality or responsibility. You've never had a lasting relationship with anyone who wasn't as weak or as helpless as yourself. So you have friends like Jimmy and me. Misfits who can't do any more than pick up your discarded clothes and empty glasses. We all hold each other up because none of us has the strength to do it alone. And lovers like Lou Tanner whose only talent is to beat your bloody face in and leave you when something better comes along. I know what I am, Evy. I don't like it and I never have. So I cover the outside with Helena Rubenstein. I use little make-up jars, you use quart bottles—and poor Jimmy uses a little of both . . . Some terrific people . . . But by some strange miracle, in there—(*Indicates bedroom*)—is a girl who is crazy in love with you because she's too young to know any better . . . But keep it up, Evy, and she'll get to know better before you can say Jack Daniels . . . The way I see it, you've got two choices. Either get a book on how to be a mature, responsible person . . . or get her out of here before you destroy her chance to become one. There's your honesty and truth, Evy. It's a perfect fit. How do you like it?

EVY   Actually, I was looking for something in a blue.

TOBY   That's the first time in my entire life I ever told anyone off. I think I'm going to be sick.

EVY   Look who's getting to be a real person. (*She goes over and puts her arms around* TOBY) Next week, with a little luck, you'll throw away the eyelashes.

TOBY   Don't hate me, Evy. I still need a little help from my friends. Tell me you don't hate me.

EVY   *Hate* you? I'm having trouble seeing you.

TOBY   So am I. But the picture's getting clearer . . . Come on, let me put something on your disgusting eye.

EVY   I got a big scene to play with Polly. I don't need an audience. Go on home.

TOBY   I can't. Marty's still there collecting some papers and things.

EVY   You want to take some advice from a drunk? Go home, wash the crap off your face, put on a sloppy house-dress and bring him a T-V dinner. What the hell could you lose?

TOBY   Nothing . . . Wouldn't it be funny if you were right?

EVY   Of course I'm right. I'm always right. That's how I got where I am today.

TOBY   Jesus, I suddenly hate my face . . . What I'd love to do is get rid of the goddamned thing.

EVY   No, you don't. You're going to send it to me by messenger. *This* lady is still in trouble.

TOBY   I'm going. *(Goes to the door)* I'm scared to death, but I'm going . . . I suddenly feel ten years older . . . Look, Evy. Look at the pretty old lady.

EVY   You'll love it. Little boys'll help you across the street.

TOBY   *(Opens the door)*   Evy, don't tell Polly the truth about what happened. Lie a little. Protect her. That's what mothers are for.

EVY   I'll say I was walking along West End Avenue and was hit by the Eastern Airlines shuttle to Boston.

TOBY   It needs work. I'll call you from home later. I have to stop off first and blow up my beauty parlor.
   (She exits, closing the door behind her. EVY *sits there a moment.* POLLY *comes out)*

POLLY   Good morning.

EVY   *(Her back to her)*   You're up. Did you get any sleep?

POLLY   No. There was terrible news on the radio. Someone was hit by an Eastern Airlines shuttle to Boston.
   (EVY *turns around and reveals herself to* POLLY)

EVY   It was me . . . How do you like it?

POLLY   Wow. It's terrific. Goes very nice with this neighborhood. Listen, I don't have any steak to put on that. Will bacon and eggs do?

EVY   You're not going to yell at me, is that it?

POLLY   I thought you were going to yell at me. I didn't go to sleep last night either. *(Suddenly* POLLY *rushes into* EVY*'s arms)* Oh, Evy, Evy, I'm so glad to see you.

EVY   *(Winces)*   The jaw, the jaw, watch the jaw.

POLLY   Listen, don't tell Toby. I promised her I wouldn't forgive you.

EVY   She's not even my friend any more. She's too old for me.

POLLY   Starting tomorrow I'm not speaking to you. But I'm so glad to see you today.

EVY   *(Pulls her to the sofa)*   You got to admit, it's not a dull place to live.

POLLY   Listen, we're not going to discuss it. It never even happened. Can I get you anything?

EVY   If you move from me, you'll get worse than I got.
     (She hugs her. There's a moment's pause)

POLLY   I had a drink.

EVY   What?

POLLY   I made myself a Scotch at two o'clock in the morning. The Excedrin P.M. wasn't working, and I had to do something to stop the throbbing in my head.

EVY   Did it stop?

POLLY No, but it made it bearable . . . Is that what it's like, Evy? Is that what it does? Make things bearable?

EVY *(Nods)* Mm-hmm. And if you take enough, it even stops the throbbing . . . Jesus, three weeks and I turned my daughter into a lush.

POLLY I hated it. I'll never take another drop in my life. From now on I'm sticking with marijuana.

EVY That's mama's good girl.

POLLY *(Pulls back)* Hey, listen, we better get moving. We have a lunch date in a half an hour, remember?

EVY What lunch date?

POLLY I told you last night. With Daddy, at Rumpel-mayer's.

EVY Are you serious? With me looking like Rocky Graziano? He'll send you to a convent.

POLLY We could put something on it. Some powder or something. Or you could wear a hat. With a little veil.

EVY I could sit behind a big screen and talk through a microphone. I can't go to Rumpelmayer's looking like this.

POLLY We'll think of something . . . How about, you just did a Tareyton commercial?

EVY How about just forgetting it?

POLLY We can't. He's expecting you. What about a pair of dark sunglasses?

EVY   It's not just the eye, baby. I have a hangover and the shakes. When I start spilling water on his lap, he's gonna notice something.

POLLY   But if you don't show up, he'll think something is wrong.

EVY   How right could things be if you show up with a punchy mother? . . . Is Melissa coming too?

POLLY   Felicia.

EVY   Felicia . . . Can you picture that scene? I walk into Rumpelmayer's looking like a dead fish, and she clicks in her coffee and he spits in his sherbet.

POLLY   She's not coming. It's just the three of us. He wants to talk to us together. I promised him that when I came here.

EVY   Well, unpromise him. I'm not going.

POLLY   *(Giving up)*   Okay . . . I'll tell him you're not feeling well. I'll figure out something. We'll do it again next week. (POLLY *goes for her coat*) In the meantime, will you see a doctor?

EVY   Yes, angel.

POLLY   When?

EVY   As soon as I look better.

POLLY   I'll bring you back a coffee malted and a toy. Get some sleep. I'll be home in an hour.
        (She opens the door, about to go)

EVY   Polly!

POLLY *(Stops; turns)* Yes?

EVY Maybe you'd better not make another date for next week . . . Not yet, anyway.

POLLY You'll be all right by next Saturday. It's not that bad, really.

EVY It's not the eye I'm worried about . . . It's the rest of the person.

POLLY *(Closes the door)* What are you saying, Mother?

EVY Nothing, baby . . . It's just that I don't know if I'm pulled together yet . . . You saw how suddenly everything unraveled yesterday . . . They warned me in the hospital that after a while I might expect some sort of setback.

POLLY Okay, you had a little setback . . . Onwards and upwards.

EVY Didn't you ever hear of downwards?

POLLY I've heard of it. You wouldn't like it there. It's worse than Garden City.

EVY Polly, I don't think I'm ready for you yet. I don't think I can handle it.

POLLY Handle what? I put on three pounds since I'm here.

EVY Mostly Sara Lee's cheesecake.

POLLY I'm alive, I'm healthy, I'm not floating on my back. What's wrong, Mother?

EVY Mother, heh? Some mother . . . When am I here? I'm out all day doing absolutely nothing and I still manage to come home late. I saw you more when you didn't live with me.

Maureen Stapleton as EVY MEARA *& Betsy von Furstenberg as* TOBY LANDAU.

POLLY   I'm not complaining.

EVY   Well, complain, damn it! What are you so forgiving for? I was a slob last night. A pig and a slob.

POLLY   It only happened once.

EVY   Wait, it's early, the new schedule didn't come out yet. Besides, it didn't happen once . . . Before last night there was an occasional beer on a wet, lonely afternoon, a couple of glasses of wine on a sunny, lonely afternoon—and once, after a really rotten Swedish movie, a double vodka.

POLLY   Okay, so forget downwards and upwards. We'll try sideways for a while.

EVY   What we'll try is that you'll go home for a couple of weeks until I pull myself together. That's all, baby, just a couple of weeks. And when you get back, I'll be a regular Doris Day type mother, okay? Freckles and everything.

POLLY   If I leave now, you know where you'll be in two weeks. You still have another eye left.

EVY   Polly, please—

POLLY   And in two weeks you'll find a reason to add another two weeks. And before you know it, Evy, I'll be all grown up and won't even need you any more.

EVY   Listen, you weren't in such bad shape when you got here.

POLLY   (Angrily)   Is it such a goddamned big deal to need somebody? If you can need a bottle of Scotch or a Lou Tanner, why can't you need me?

EVY   I do need you, baby. I just don't want to use you. Like the rest of the company around here . . . In a few weeks you'll know the regular routine. You'll get a two-hour storm warning, then wait in your bedroom until all the bottles are empty and all the glasses are smashed, and in the mornings there'll be a lot of Alka-Seltzers and black coffee and crying and forgiving and promises, and we'll live happily ever after for two more weeks. And in a year or so you won't even mind it. Like Jimmy and Toby . . . But they have nothing better to do with their lives. You're only seventeen.

POLLY   They're just friends. I'm your daughter.

EVY   You get my point?

POLLY   No! . . . What *is* it, Evy? Am I getting kicked out because you're afraid I'm going to grow up to be a crutch instead of a person? Or do you just want to be left alone so there's no one here to lock up the liquor cabinet?

EVY   You're going to be late for Rumpelmayer's.

POLLY   *Screw* Rumpelmayer's!

EVY   *(Looks at* POLLY *and smiles)* My, my . . . Look how quickly you can learn if you pay attention.

POLLY   I'm sorry.

EVY   Go on. Please, Polly. Go now.

POLLY   Don't I get to argue my side?

EVY   Not today. Mother is hung over.

POLLY   I see . . . Okay . . . If the room's not for rent, it's not for rent . . . When do you want me out?

EVY   All right, let's not get maudlin. You're not moving to the Philippines, just 86th and Madison.

POLLY *(Nods)*   I'll be back for my stuff later.

EVY   I'll get everything ready. If nothing else, I'm a terrific packer.

POLLY   I'm glad you finally found something to keep you busy.
   (She glares at EVY, *then crosses to the door. She turns and looks at* EVY*)*

EVY *(A pause)*   What?

POLLY   I was just wondering if you were going to say good-bye.

EVY   Not unless you want to see a major breakdown.

POLLY   Never mind. It's the thought that counts.
   (The phone rings. POLLY *exits, closing the door behind her.* EVY *is at her low ebb. She crosses to her mink coat and takes out a pint bottle of liquor. She pours it into a glass and sits down on a chair, her legs up on a stool. The phone stops ringing. She drinks. After a moment the doorbell rings. She pays no attention. We hear* JIMMY*'s voice)*

JIMMY   Evy? . . . Evy, it's Jimmy . . . Evy, I know you're there. I just saw Polly on the stairs. *(She drinks)* Damn it, Evy, answer me.

EVY   Evy's not here. She moved. This is a recording.

JIMMY *(Pounds on the door)*   Evy, I'll break this door down, I swear . . . I know what you're doing in there. *(A pause)* Three seconds, Evy. If it's not open in three seconds, I'm breaking it down.

(She drinks. Suddenly the door breaks down and JIMMY'S *body hurtles into the room and onto the floor.* EVY *looks at him)*

EVY   Jesus, I didn't think you could do it.

JIMMY *(Gets up, moves to her)*   I knew it. I knew you'd be here with a glass in your hand drinking yourself—*(He notices her eye)* Oh, my God. Look at you. Look at your face.

EVY   If you're going to throw up, use the bathroom.

JIMMY   He beat you. The son of a bitch beat you.

EVY   And if you try to take this away from me, I'll show you how it was done.

JIMMY   It was Lou Tanner, wasn't it? Toby just called me. I'll find him. If it takes me the rest of my life, I'll track that son of a bitch down and kill him.

EVY   Once he hears, he'll never sleep another night . . . Will you close the drapes, Jimmy? And then leave me alone like a good boy.

JIMMY *(He closes the drapes)*   Sure. I'll leave you alone. I turn my back for two seconds, they have to call the emergency squad. What happened? How did he beat you?

EVY   How many ways are there? You get hit and you fall down.

JIMMY   Look at your eye. What did he hit you with, his guitar?

EVY   No, the guitar was the preliminaries.

JIMMY   I want to know the details, Evy. How did he beat you?

EVY   Since when are you interested in sports?
      (In a fit of anger, he pushes her)

JIMMY   You think it's so goddamned funny—go look at yourself.

EVY   How come everybody's so physical lately? Where were you all when I needed you?

JIMMY   Have you called the police? Have you seen a doctor? What have you done?

EVY   Outside of bleeding, not very much. You want the goddamned case, I give it to you. If you're interested in my welfare, get me another glass, then turn out the light and get out of here. Leave me alone, Jimmy, please . . .

JIMMY   I'll never forgive myself for running out last night. Never. *(He turns off the alcove light. He goes back to* EVY *on the sofa, and puts his arm on her)* It's all right, baby . . . We got through it before, we'll get through it again.

EVY   And again . . . and again . . .

JIMMY   Feel better?

EVY   Much . . . There was this movie with Jean Simmons.

JIMMY   English or American?

EVY   English. And she was in love with this boy.

JIMMY   Stewart Granger? David Niven? Michael Wilding?

EVY   He was very short with blond hair.

JIMMY   Short English actor. Blond hair. Alec Guinness? Michael Caine?

EVY   Miles? Mills?

JIMMY   Mills. John Mills. *Great Expectations,* directed by David Lean, with Valerie Hobson, John Mills, Francis Sullivan, and introducing Jean Simmons. What about it?

EVY   She had this crazy old aunt who spent forty years in a wedding dress. The boy she loved never showed up for the wedding. Never saw him again but she never changed a thing for forty years. Cobwebs on the goddamned wedding cake. And she never went out into the city and she closed all the shutters and never let the sun into the house. She was covered with dust, this crazy old broad. Sat there in the dark, rotting and falling apart . . . Mice nibbling away at the wedding gifts . . . And as I watched her I remembered saying to myself, "She doesn't seem so crazy to me."

JIMMY   Martita Hunt played the aunt. Her dress caught fire and she burned to death, screaming on the floor. Try not to think of it.

EVY   I'm okay. There ain't no cobwebs on me.

JIMMY   What can I get you? Let me get you something. Coffee? A sandwich? Something to drink? I'll even let you have a real drink, how about that?

EVY   It's no fun that way. I have to sneak it.

JIMMY   If I go away, if I leave you alone, will you take a nap?

EVY   For you? Anything.

JIMMY   Not for me. For yourself.

EVY   Well, we'll split it. I'll sleep a little for you and a little for me . . . Will you turn the rest of the lights out? (JIMMY *crosses and turns out another light*) I can still see you, Charley. *(He turns out the remaining light. The room is almost in total darkness, except for the light in the kitchen)* That's better.
     (JIMMY *moves in the dark and stumbles against a stool*)

JIMMY   Christ, now I can't find the door.

EVY   Don't worry about it, darling. Come to bed.

JIMMY   Bitch, go to sleep. *(He has found the door and opens it)* I'll take a walk in Central Park. If I'm not back in an hour, I found true happiness.
     (He goes, closing the door behind him)

EVY   And get something for me, you bastard.
     (She is alone. She gets up, crosses to the record player and switches on the record again. Her voice is heard, singing the song from last night. She pours herself another drink and goes back to the piano, drinking and listening. Suddenly the front door opens and POLLY *stands there in the doorway, looking worriedly into the dark room)*

POLLY *(Concerned)*   Mother? Are you all right?

EVY *(In the shadows)*   What are you doing here?
     (She gets up quickly)

POLLY   I forgot my wallet. I don't have carfare . . . What's the matter with the lights?

EVY   Nothing. I have a headache.

POLLY   Well, no wonder. It's so depressing in here. Like some ghost movie on the late show.

EVY *(Turns off the record player)* Great Expectations, directed by David Lean. (POLLY *switches on a light.* EVY *winces from the glare)* Christ, do you have to do that?

POLLY   I have to find my wallet. I'll be out in a minute. (POLLY *starts to look around and then finds the half-empty liquor bottle on the table where* EVY *was sitting. She holds up the bottle, turns and looks at* EVY)

EVY   Well, if that's your wallet, take it and go.

POLLY   It's not my wallet. It looks like yours.

EVY   All right, what do you want, a reward? Put it down and go. Can't you see I'm trying to take a nap?

POLLY   Some nap.
(She turns on another light and then another lamp)

EVY   What are you doing? I don't want those lights on. Leave those lights alone.

POLLY   So you can sit here in the dark, drinking?

EVY   It's not hard, I know where my lips are. (POLLY *goes to the windows)* Get away from those curtains.

POLLY *(Opening one curtain)* Sitting here in the dark like some crazy spook. I have a crazy spook for a mother.

EVY   And I have a disrespectful pain in the ass for a daughter. That's what I get for sending you to a private school.

POLLY *(Opening the other curtains)* Why don't you get some bats and owls in here? Fly around the room on a broomstick. Crazy old spook mother.

EVY   Where's my pocketbook? Take a taxi, buy a car—only get out of here.

POLLY   And you can sit here and finish the rest of the bottle, right?

EVY   I wasn't drinking, I was meditating.

POLLY   Ten more minutes and you'd have meditated right out on the floor. That's why you want to be alone.

EVY   I'm not alone. Jimmy was here. And he's coming back in an hour.

POLLY   And he'll do whatever you ask him, right? Turn out the lights, seal up the windows, refill your bottles? Anything as long as Evy's happy.

EVY   Yes! Yes, dammit! Now get out of here and leave me alone!

POLLY   That's why you kicked me out. Because you're afraid of me. Aren't you, Mother? Admit you're afraid of me.

EVY   Don't test me. One more word, you'll walk into Rumpelmayer's looking like me.

POLLY   Go ahead, hit me. I don't mind a little pain, Mother. It sure beats indifference!

EVY   Jesus, you can't say a word around here without you listening at the door.

POLLY   I don't have to listen through the door. When you're drunk, they can hear you in Brazil.

EVY   I won't stand for this kind of talk.

POLLY   Yes, you will. You'll stand for anything!

EVY   Stop it! Stop it, Polly!

POLLY   Then *make* me! Do something about it!

EVY   I won't be talked to this way. I swear, you're going to get it, Polly.

POLLY   I'm waiting. Please! Give it to me. Evy!

EVY   Not from me. From your father. I swear to God, I'm going to tell your father.

POLLY   *(Yells)   Then tell him!* Tell him what I've become after three weeks. You want things to tell him about, Evy? *(Picks up a glass)* Here! *(She hurls it against the bookcase, smashing it to pieces)* All right? Now come to Rumpelmayer's and tell him . . . Only please don't sit in the dark for the rest of your life.
   (POLLY *has burst into tears. She kneels, crying.* EVY *finds it difficult to go to her. It is quiet for a moment)*

EVY   Couldn't he have picked a nice out-of-the-way restaurant in Nebraska?

POLLY   *(Turns around hopefully)*   You mean you've changed your mind?

EVY   I didn't change anything.

POLLY   All right, don't change your mind. Just change your dress. You can change your mind on the way over.

EVY   *(Looks to heaven)*   She's *his* daughter. I have too much class for a daughter like this.

POLLY   Listen, how about if I don't come back as a daughter? I could be a house guest. I'll just stay till I'm thirty-five, then get out. I promise.

EVY   Didn't we just settle all that?

POLLY You and your daughter settled all that. I'm a stranger. Why don't you show me the rest of the apartment?

EVY *(Again, up to heaven)* Who is she? Who sent this monster to torment me?

POLLY Felicia. She can't stand any of us.
(POLLY *has clearly won.* EVY *wilts and opens her arms.*
POLLY *runs in*)

EVY Oh, God, I'm not strong enough to resist you . . . I suppose I'll be speaking at your school next week.

POLLY We've got fifteen minutes. What can we do with your face in fifteen minutes?

EVY Christ, I don't know. There's a one-hour cleaners around the corner.

POLLY You've known Toby Landau for twelve years and you never heard of make-up? Come on, sit down.

EVY We'll never get away with it.

POLLY Yes, you will.
(She takes out a compact from her purse)

EVY I'll get twenty years for impersonating a mother.

POLLY Good. We'll share a cell together.

EVY The hell we will. I'm forty-three years old. Someday I'm getting my own place.
(POLLY *starts to apply make-up under the eye*)

POLLY Now remember. Once we get there, don't be nervous. Just be cool and nonchalant.

EVY   What if I do something stupid like eat the ice cream with a fork?

POLLY   Then I'll eat mine with a fork. He'll look at us, think *he's* wrong, and eat *his* with a fork . . . Try not to move.

EVY   Who would believe this? A middle-aged drunk with a black eye is worried about impressing a forty-seven-year-old spitter.

POLLY   All right, I'm through.

EVY   How does it look?

POLLY   Much better.

EVY   *(Picks up the compact and looks at herself)*   It's *not* better. It looks like I was punched in the eye and someone put make-up on it.

POLLY   If we don't get away with it, we'll tell him the truth. He's a terrific person, Evy. He'll understand the truth.

EVY   About Lou Tanner?

POLLY   No. The Eastern Airlines shuttle to Boston. Come on. Let's get a decent dress on you. You look like you're collecting for UNICEF.

EVY   Polly.

POLLY   What?

EVY   When I grow up, I want to be just like you.

Curtain